AWAKENING THE HIDDEN STORYTELLER

ROBIN MOORE

Awakening the Hidden Storyteller

How to Build a Storytelling Tradition in Your Family

SHAMBHALA
Boston
1991

This book is dedicated to my grandfather, George Baer,
who can still tell a good story.

Shambhala Publications, Inc.
Horticultural Hall
300 Massachusetts Avenue
Boston, Massachusetts 02115

© 1991 by Robin Moore
Photographs by Les Rudnick
Design by Diane Levy

Excerpts from *Angling in America* by Charles Goodspeed,
copyright 1939 by Charles E. Goodspeed, copyright ©
renewed 1967 by George T. Goodspeed. Reprinted by
permission of Houghton Mifflin Co.

9 8 7 6 5 4 3

Printed in the United States of America on acid-free paper ♾

Distributed in the United States by Random House and in
Canada by Random House of Canada Ltd.

Library of Congress Cataloging-in-Publication Data

Moore, Robin.
    Awakening the hidden storyteller: how to build a
storytelling tradition in your family / Robin Moore.
        p.   cm.
    Includes bibliographical references.
    ISBN 0-87773-599-9
    1. Storytelling.   2. Storytelling—Study and teaching.
3. Family recreation.   I. Title.
LB1042.M59   1991   90-53531
808.5'43—dc20   CIP

CONTENTS

Inside each of us is a natural-born storyteller, waiting to be released. For some of us, this inner storyteller may be silent or sleeping or simply hidden from view. This book aims to awaken the hidden storyteller in you and to guide you and your family in building a storytelling tradition at home.

The techniques you'll find here are ones I have developed over the past ten years in my work as a professional storyteller and as a teacher of workshops on storytelling skills. My primary storytelling experience, though, has been as a parent, so the real testing ground for these ideas has been in the imagination of my own kids. Because I wanted to make sure that this book would be useful to families at home, I asked my son and daughter to test-pilot the explorations in it. Although the book is aimed at parents of elementary-school-aged kids, its content is easily adaptable for families with children of any age, as well as for classrooms. This is not, however, a conventional workbook or textbook, nor is it for the armchair enthusiast. Instead, it's more of a guidebook to the landscape of the imagination.

In the voyages we'll be taking together, you and your family will have an opportunity to explore the imaginative world, just as if we were taking off to explore a blank space on the map.

By making this book highly participatory, I hope to help you to avoid one of the major pitfalls of parenting self-help books: While you are reading the book, you are not doing what is really important—you are not spending time with your kids. As in:

Son: Dad, can you play with me?

Father: Not right now, Johnny. I'm reading a book on effective parenting.

This book is designed for you and your kids to enjoy together. I hope your family finds these voyages as entertaining and rewarding as mine has.

ACKNOWLEDGMENTS

Experiences from many lives have contributed to the making of this book. I'd like to express my thanks to those who have helped me:

To my parents, grandparents, and relatives, who filled my boyhood days with stories. Now you know: I was really listening.

To my children, Jesse and Rachel, for their perfect interruptions, without which this book would never have been written. To my wife, Jacque, for her unwavering confidence in my ability.

To my comrades: the storytellers, writers, thinkers, and dreamers who have nurtured me along the way.

To my students and my clients, who have made it possible for me to pursue this profession through their loyalty and support.

This book is the special effort of many people. Thanks to my editor at Shambhala, Kendra Crossen, and to my agent, Barrie Van Dyck.

A special thanks to photographer Les Rudnick, whose pictures appear in this volume. His "fly on the wall" technique in our workshops was most effective.

Les took the photos at a workshop at Open Connections, Inc., a parent resource center in Bryn Mawr, Pennsylvania, hosted by Peter Bergson. Thanks, Peter, for facilitating that and many other workshops at Open Connections.

Thanks to the families who tested this book and offered suggestions, comments, and companionship as we translated workshop exercises into written form. They are Peter, Emily, Julia, and Nicholas Bergson-Shilcock; Joel, Melissa, Abbie, Philip, and Lucy Huff; Susan, Keith, and Steven Kleinman; Nicholas, Jackie, Tony, Megan, and Deborah Lemieur; G.B., David, Christine, and Helen Roberts; Meyer, Daniel, and Rebecca Rothbart; William, Delia, Melody, and Judy Tash.

Additional thanks to the many friends of storytelling who have contributed encouragement. To all those who have helped along the way but whose names don't appear here, know that I am deeply grateful.

AWAKENING THE HIDDEN STORYTELLER

The Mythic Truth

When I was a boy growing up in the mountains of central Pennsylvania, I used to spend summers with my grandfather at a place called Silver Lake. He and my grandmother had built a cottage there during the Great Depression. As far as I know, it was the only luxury they ever allowed themselves.

My grandfather loved fishing. Summers, when I was with him, he took me fishing almost every day.

I remember one day we were out on the boat fishing when I caught a great big lake trout. I hauled him into the boat, and I was just taking the hook out of his lower jaw when I made the mistake of looking that fish in the eye. Now, I had looked into many fishes' eyes before, but I had never seen one that had looked back at me. What I saw was a gleam of intelligence that I had never seen in a fish's eye before.

I said, "Grandpa, look at this."

My grandfather set down his rod and examined the fish. The three of us sat there, looking at each other. My grandfather worked the hook out of the fish's mouth and dumped him into a bailing bucket full of water.

"What did you do that for?" I asked.

My grandfather looked out across the lake, "Well, old-timer, you're too young to remember this, but about ten years ago, your uncle Jimmy caught a lake trout that was so smart, he was able to bring him up on the land to do tricks like a dog. Could be, that fish was related to this one. What do you say, old-timer, should we give 'er a try?"

How could I refuse?

We paddled back to land, tied up the boat, and carried the bucket with the fish around to an old-fashioned rain barrel full of water. My grandfather dumped that fish in, and he swam around just fine.

That night, after that fish was asleep, my grandfather sneaked out to that rain barrel carrying an empty bucket. Being careful not to wake that fish, he dipped out a bucketful of water and dumped it on the ground.

Every night, while that fish was asleep, my grandfather would dip out another bucket of water. After about a week that barrel was almost empty, with just a little puddle of water on the bottom.

I remember the very first morning we took him out of the barrel. There was a real heavy dew on the grass that morning. My grandfather gently lifted the fish out of the barrel and laid him in the dew. That moisture was just enough to keep that fish alive.

My grandfather got down on his hands and knees a few feet away from that fish. He motioned to the little guy, saying, "Come on, boy, come to me."

Darned if that fish didn't wiggle across the grass toward my grandfather.

"Grandpa, what's he doing?" I asked.

"Well, what do you think he's doin'? He's obeyin' my commands."

I could see that my grandfather was excited. He and that fish played around on the lawn for about an hour before the sun started to dry out the grass and we figured we had better put him back in the barrel.

Every morning, while the dew was still on the grass, my grandfather and I would get up at dawn and train that fish.

It was after our first week of training that I had to go away to Boy Scout camp for two weeks.

When I came back, I couldn't wait to see that fish.

I remember I was walking down the dirt road toward the cottage when I saw my grandfather, walking toward me across the grass. And there, walking beside him, balanced up on his tail fins, was that fish.

I was flabbergasted. "How did you do it?" I asked.

"Oh, it just took a little training," he said modestly.

Well, we had quite a summer with that fish. After that, he could go anywhere with us. We'd go for a walk, that fish would go with us. We'd go down to the grocery store, that fish would go with us.

We even took him fishing. We made him a little tiny fishing pole out of the end of a broken rod, and we put some line on it and a hook. (Of course, we had to help him bait the hooks.) And he would stand up on his hind fins in the boat, we would put that little fishing pole under his front fin, and he caught a lot of fish.

Then, one day, late in August, something terrible happened.

The three of us were out in the boat, fishing. Suddenly I heard this terrible splash. I turned around and looked, but the fish was gone. He had lost his balance and fallen overboard.

"Quick, get him, he'll drown!" my grandfather hollered.

I was in Boy Scouts. I knew what to do. I tore the sneakers off my feet and leaped overboard. I could see that fish, sinking like a rock. I swam down and scooped him up, brought him up to the surface, and handed him to my grandfather. He laid him in the bottom of the boat and hauled me aboard.

That poor fish coughed and choked. He had swallowed a lot of water.

My grandfather had to bend down and give him mouth-to-gill resuscitation to bring him back.

That night, when the fish was safely asleep in his barrel, my grandfather took me aside.

"We never shoulda done it," he said. "We never shoulda taken him out of the water. It just goes to show, you just can't go against nature." Then he looked up at me. "Old-timer, we gotta get that fish back in the lake where he belongs."

So every evening, while that fish was asleep, my grandfather would sneak out to that rain barrel with a full bucket of water. Every night, he would pour in a bucketful.

After a week or so, that barrel was completely full and that fish had learned to breathe again in the water.

On the very last day of my summer vacation, we took that fish, put him in a bucket, and rowed far and away out into the center of the lake.

We just sat, listening to the water lap up against the side of the boat. At that hour, just as the sun was dipping down, all the lake was a mirror. I could see everything reflected in its surface:

I saw a blue sky with clouds drifting by. A chevron of wild geese flew over, honking. I could see the willows that hung their arms in the water. I could see the boat, and I could see my grandfather, and I could see me.

It was then that I realized: the summer was over.

I guess my grandfather was thinking the same thing I was. We just sat there for a long time, not wanting to let that fish go, not wanting to let the summer go, but knowing we had to. Then my grandfather gestured to the bucket.

"Give me a hand with this, old-timer. Let's send this fella back where he belongs."

We dumped that fish overboard, and he swam away a graceful sliver of silver, and that was the last I ever saw of him.

That was one of the last times I saw my grandfather, too, because he died a little bit after that.

But they say those lake trout live a long time. And sometimes I wonder if that fish is still out there, swimming around. And sometimes I wonder if he thinks of me and remembers me, like I remember him.

As long as I live, I'll never forget that fish.

THE GIFT OF GAB

When I was a boy, I heard a lot of stories like that. On summer evenings at my grandparents' cottage at Silver Lake, the relatives would sit out on the lawn under the willow trees, eating field-fresh corn and salty German pretzels, and drinking Iron City beer out of tall, cool glasses. Then they would tell stories: not just tall tales, but true ones, too.

They would tell how my grandparents had snuck off to Maryland when they were in their late teens and gotten married in secret. How they had returned and lived in their parents' houses for weeks before anyone found out.

How my aunt Bee and my grandmother would get disgusted with the men every winter and take off for Florida to get some sand in their shoes when the long Pennsylvania winters got them down.

How my uncle Al was killed in the Harrisburg Switching Yard while working for the Pennsylvania Railroad, crushed between two railcars because of a wrong signal given by his own brother.

Or how my father used to court my mother from that very same cottage, when he would paddle by in his kayak on moonlit nights and offer to take her out and show her the constellations. "You can see them a lot better from the center of the lake," he would say.

A boy could learn a lot, simply by sitting and listening—especially when the grownups thought he wasn't. From these talkative people I learned about the magic of the spoken word and the simple pleasure of telling stories. My family were hardworking folk who had lived through the Great Depression and the two world wars. They'd hunted and fished and driven bread trucks and baked bread and birthed babies. They had a native intelligence about them; they had "the gift of gab."

They didn't call what they did storytelling. To them it was only talk. It wasn't just any kind of talk, though: it was that sweet, slow, meandering, nutritious talk that isn't headed anywhere and doesn't care if it gets there. It was talk that had no ambitions for itself. The purpose of their talk was not to teach a lesson (although a lesson could be learned from it). Nor was it their purpose to prove a point or convey a "message." It was just talk for the pure pleasure of talking.

I heard stories in my own home, too. My mother and father told stories to my brothers and sisters and me all the years we were growing up. Later on, I joined the Boy Scout troop in our little town and heard stories in the best setting of all: by a blazing campfire, under the dome of a great star-sprinkled sky. I enjoyed all the stories I learned when I was a kid, but I didn't have an inkling of how important they would become for me later on.

When I was eighteen, I enlisted in the army, fought in the Vietnam War, and came home to go to college on the G.I. Bill at Pennsylvania State University. I majored in journalism, under the vague notion that I wanted to be a writer. After graduation, I met my wife, Jacque, and married her. I left central Pennsylvania to take a job as a writer for a business magazine in suburban Philadelphia. Judging from outward appearances, I was a successful young man: happily married with a child on the way, a nice mortgaged home in the suburbs, and a well-paying job. Still, a vague feeling that said "This is not it" gnawed at me.

Then one day, while driving to work, I heard someone on the radio telling stories. That changed everything. In the brief interview that followed the stories, I learned that this storyteller actually earned a living by performing at schools, libraries, and festivals.

It was as if a thunderbolt had ripped through the roof of the car and split me wide open. My first thought was: "I didn't know you were allowed to do that." My second thought was: "This is it!"

Later that day I called the radio station and learned that there was not just one but five people in the Philadelphia area who made their living solely by telling stories. A few weeks later I went to a gathering at the home of one of the tellers and found out about the National Association for the Preservation and Perpetuation of Storytelling (NAPPS) in Jonesborough, Tennessee. I learned that there were professional storytellers all over the country. At the National Storytelling Festival that fall, I felt as if I were swept up by a thunderstorm. In the space of a weekend, I met several professional tellers who were telling stories at schools, festivals, prisons, churches, and theaters, and on radio and television. Everyone at the festival talked about the storytelling renaissance, an awakening interest in storytelling that was spreading quickly throughout the country. When the festival ended, I drove all night from Tennessee to Pennsylvania with the voices of the tellers in my ears. I knew I would never be the same again.

When I told Jacque that I planned to become a professional storyteller, I expected some resistance. She had seen how restless I was in the nine-to-five world, though, and she had confidence—perhaps more than I did—that I would succeed.

A year later, I left my job and started telling stories for a modest fee at local schools, libraries, and scout meetings. It wasn't hard to find stories to tell; I simply dusted off the stories I had heard when I was a boy: American Indian legends, animal stories, and hunting and fishing tales. The response far exceeded my expectations. I saw that telling stories was a valuable skill. My business prospered. Within a year I had equaled the income from my writing job.

Meanwhile, I was learning about storytelling at home as well. I told my son and daughter stories, just as my parents had told me stories. When my children learned to speak, they began telling their own stories, with grace and skill. I never taught my kids storytelling; they just learned it, as I had from my own family.

TEACHING STORYTELLING

After I had been a working storyteller for a few years, I got a call from the local adult school, asking me to teach a series of four evening workshops to parents and teachers about telling stories to children. Not realizing how poorly qualified I was to do that, I readily accepted.

I arrived on the first night of class with a simple plan: I would tell a few stories to get the ball rolling. Then we would go around the room, round-robin fashion, allowing each person to tell a story while I gave tips on improving the telling. What could be simpler?

As it turned out, it wasn't simple at all. The people who signed up for the course, parents and grandparents, didn't seem to have a clear idea of what storytelling was. Many of them had never gotten stories in their own childhood and felt frustrated in their attempts to create something for their children that they had never had. When I asked them to recall stories they heard as a child, many drew a blank.

I realized that if I was going to give these people what they wanted, I would have to go back to basics. I was going to have to go back and consciously think through a process I had learned unconsciously. I was going to have to go back into the machinery of things and find out what makes storytelling work, then devise a plan for passing that skill along to others.

Somehow, nature took over. As I fumbled along, the natural process of storytelling began to take hold. One of my early discoveries was that many people saw stories as words to be memorized and delivered, like a book report. Instinctively, I knew this was wrong. For a story to come alive, I knew that the teller must "see" the story taking place in the imagination, in the same way that we experience a dream, and then convey that sense of vitality to the listener. As a way of avoiding the "book report" syndrome, I asked the students to put away their storybooks and tell stories from personal experience.

The effect was immediate and stunning. The same fellow who stumbled through a memorized version of "The Three Little Pigs" told a complex and touching story about a rail-car trip he had taken with his father through the Pacific Northwest when he was a boy. A woman told of a close call with a stray dog. A young mother told about how her son was born in a hospital elevator on the way to the maternity ward. All of us were astonished at the power and clarity of these tales.

In the weeks that followed, it was all I could do to keep up with the things my students were "learning" from me about storytelling. We ended the course with a real sense of accomplishment.

Encouraged by my success, I went on and taught other courses. I became fascinated with the study of the human imagination. I wanted to know, both for my students and for myself, what made it work.

I read a mountain of books on psychology, anthropology, and mythology. I took workshops on dream appreciation, shamanism, and guided visualization. I sought out other storytellers, both amateurs and professionals, to try to figure out what made them good or bad. And I forged ahead, "teaching" storytelling workshops, trusting that the process of teaching would reveal some of the secrets of the storyteller's world.

Eventually, I was able to distill what I learned into a workshop of my own, one that allows people to reclaim and use their natural storytelling abilities. Ten years later, I find myself writing this book, as a way of passing along what I have learned.

ABOUT THIS BOOK

The first two chapters of this book guide you through a series of "voyages" that help you to assemble the storyteller's tool kit. Storytellers use inner and outer tools. Inner tools (chapter 1) include memory, imagination, and visualization. Outer tools (chapter 2) include voice, gesture, and movement. Chapter 3 focuses on locating, selecting, and preparing story sources, the raw materials for your tales.

The book's voyages are journeys in the imagination to be taken with eyes closed, alone or with a partner or, ideally, with the whole family. When we return from these inner voyages, we can tell our stories just as we do when we return from geographical journeys. These imaginative expeditions are worthwhile in themselves, but each, in addition, teaches important storytelling skills.

The commentary that follows each voyage will help you fit the experience of the voyage into a larger context. It gives views from the fields of mythology, psychology, and anthropology on how the skills you have learned in this voyage fit into the larger picture. Follow-up information also includes comments from parents and kids who have test-piloted this book.

A cautionary word here: simply reading about a voyage is no substitute for taking your own. In truth, you can't teach storytelling any more than you can teach parenting. Being a storyteller, like being a parent, means mastering a constellation of skills, learned by experience. That's why the approach of this book is experiential.

If you voyage with your children, be sure to give them equal time to tell their own stories. Pay special attention to how they tell stories, to see what you can learn about storytelling from them. The real benefit of taking these voyages with our children may be simply to bring us adults up to their imaginative level.

In the remainder of the book, chapters 5 and 6, you will embark on a wide range of voyages using your new skills. These family-centered story activities relate to time-travel, tribal lore, and ecology.

The extensive resource section will provide you with information on books, tapes, and other publications. It includes a list of national and regional storytelling organizations, festivals, and conferences.

STORYTELLING TODAY

Storytelling has been hauled down out of the attic and given a place in the home again. The storytelling renaissance I learned about in 1979 is still going on. When I went to my first NAPPS festival, some ten years ago, it was the only one of its kind. Today there are more than one hundred annual storytelling festivals nationwide. In 1989, the thirteenth annual NAPPS festival reported an attendance of six thousand—a twenty percent jump over the previous year's attendance. Storytelling conferences and workshops are growing at a record rate. Several colleges now offer graduate courses in storytelling. Ten years ago, only a handful of people were making a living by telling stories. Today, there are over three hundred full-time tellers nationwide. Tale-spinning has become a legitimate career choice.

While NAPPS has led the storytelling movement on the national level, an impressive network of local guilds and story-swapping groups has also sprung up. These informal local groups publish newsletters and give concerts.

People outside the storytelling community have noticed this flurry of activity. The publishing world has recognized the trend. A decade ago there were only a half-dozen storytelling how-to's in print. Books like *The Way of the Storyteller* by Ruth Sawyer and *The Art of the Storyteller* by Marie Shedlock offered solid advice from a librarian's perspective on the storyteller's craft. The American library system deserves a great deal of credit for keeping storytelling alive during the "dark ages" when radio, movies, and television began to silence the front-porch storyteller. Today, a dozen new books each year introduce readers to the storyteller's world. A new and exciting wave of books by psychologists, educational specialists, artists, and theologians use the tools of the storyteller to understand life in postindustrial society.

Storytelling has entered mainstream culture through radio shows like Garrison Keillor's "Prairie Home Companion" and "American Radio Theater." Full-length motion pictures like *My Dinner with André* and Spalding Gray's *Swimming to Cambodia* experiment with storytelling as a cinematic form. The phenomenal success of *The Power of Myth,* a PBS television series presented by Joseph Campbell and Bill Moyers, has made Campbell's book *The Hero's Journey* a best-seller again after thirty-five years.

Storytelling can play an important role in the 1990s, the Decade of the Environment. The first step in rethinking our place on the planet should be reconnecting with our inner landscape. Then we will better relate to the landscape of the planet.

STORYTELLING AT HOME

While much has been written in other books about the educational and psychological aspects of storytelling, this book focuses on telling stories at home with the family. You can, of course, easily adapt these voyages for use in schools, libraries, churches, or social groups, too. Even though I tell stories for a living, it is the storytelling I do at home that I value most. I can't imagine our family life without storytelling.

As our ancestors knew very well, storytelling adds a layer of richness to everyday life. Stories become real for us, and simple objects—trees or candles or rocks—take on special meanings because we have encountered them in our stories. When I tell my kids a story like "Silver Lake Trout," they know that some of it really happened and some of it didn't. They know that a story doesn't have to be true in the literal sense. They also know that I am not trying to deceive them or trick them. What we seek in storytelling is mythic truth. A myth is, as the mythologist Jean Houston says, "something that never happened but is going on all the time." The Jungian analyst Robert Johnson points out, "A myth is something that is true on the inside but not on the outside." Although the story of the walking fish is not factually true, it is an accurate reflection of how I felt about my grandfather and our summers at Silver Lake. When my kids hear this story, they get a glimpse into a time before they were born, a time they somehow come out of. This story gives them a link to me and to their great-grandfather, who died before they were born. Storytelling, creating an imaginative world and investing it with meaning, has added a great strength and joy to our family's life.

In an essay on the importance of story, the noted psychologist and author James Hillman comments, "I have tried to show in my work how adult and child have come to be set against each other: childhood tends to mean wonder, imagination, creative spontaneity, while adulthood [tends to mean] the loss of these perspectives. So, the first task, as I see it, is re-storying the adult—the teacher and the parent and the grandparent—in order to restore the imagination to the primary place in consciousness in each of us, regardless of age."

This re-storying and restoring of the imaginative world is what my book is all about. Storytelling, the ancient human skill, is the tool.

We stand now on the threshold of adventure. Inner space is, for many of us, unexplored territory. Even the most experienced world travelers have seen only a little of the vastness of the human imagination. In *The Hero's Journey*, Joseph Campbell describes several steps that all journeys have in common. The first step is what he calls "The Call of Adventure." You have heard the Call of Adventure now. So let's plunge ahead in our quest to awaken the hidden storyteller.

CHAPTER 1

Venturing In

Opening
the Storehouse
of Memory
and Creativity

In this chapter we will:

- Establish a time and place for telling stories at home.
- Experience, through a series of voyages, the complete story-telling process from the source of the story in the teller's mind to the final story in the listener's mind.
- Examine several stories of true-life experiences, with special attention to the storyteller's inner tools.

Let's begin our voyages by establishing a time and place for storytelling that will fit into the rhythm of your family's life. Make it easy on yourself and enter these voyages with the spirit of the adventurer.

THE TIME

If your family is like most that I know, time is at a premium for you. Think carefully about the flow of your family's daily and weekly life, and identify blocks of time when you are all together and in the mood for adventure. If you are working on this book alone, the same idea applies. Choosing the time of day is an important consideration. Bedtime, the traditional time for stories, is not always ideal for our voyages, since these adventures stimulate the imagination and can lead to long discussions and additional activities. Still, these voyages are best undertaken in subdued light, so many families choose a time in the early evening, after dinner.

One family found time for voyaging by stealing it from TV watching: "What we did sounds crazy, but it really worked," said the mother. "We told the kids that instead of watching TV on weeknights, we would do our voyages. But we promised them that on the nights when we did watch the tube, we would really pig out. We would make a bowl of popcorn, spread blankets and pillows on the floor, and be really decadent. Since then, TV watching has become an event rather than a habit."

Another family stole time from dinner preparation by making every Thursday take-out pizza night and using the "found" time for their voyaging.

THE PLACE

As we progress, we will be taking our storytelling with us everywhere we go—in the car or outdoors, for example—but at first you should choose a place in the home to voyage from and use that space consistently. Select a comfortable room that is free from distractions. You should have enough space for everyone to lie flat on the floor. A rug on the floor is a good idea. A low light level is also a plus. Prepare the room by drawing the shades, turning off the radio and TV, and unplugging the phone.

For our initial voyage, we are going to seat everyone on the floor so that we see the room from a different perspective. Next we are going to bring some fire into the room. The simplest and safest way to do this is with a candle. If you use the dripless kind, it will eliminate any cleanup. An ordinary dining room candle holder will work fine. Place a dinner plate under the candle holder as an added precaution against spilled wax. Have matches on hand to light the candle and a wristwatch with a sweep second hand.

THE LEADER

We are nearly ready to take our first voyage. Before you actually take the voyage, though, read the voyage instructions through. You may want to choose one person to be the voyage leader. It is the leader's responsibility to prepare the room and read the instructions. For the first voyage, choose an adult for this job. Later, you can involve the kids in the process. If you are working alone, the voyages will be slightly more challenging. Read the instructions over carefully and work from memory. Though most of the voyages are done with the eyes closed, you may need to peek at the book occasionally.

VOYAGE 1

Lighting the Flame

TIME: 10 minutes

GOAL: To create a special spot in the house where the family can settle in and slip the bonds of ordinary, everyday reality; to use a candle flame as a physical and emotional centerpiece.

PREPARATION: Prepare the room and have on hand a candle, matches, and a wristwatch.

INSTRUCTIONS:

- The leader lights the candle and notes the time.
- The leader says, "Let's sit quietly and enjoy the light of our candle."
- During the ten-minute period you need not be absolutely silent, but do not talk the whole time either. Let silence come into the room. If you speak, do it quietly. Allow the family to settle into the silence and the candlelight.
- When exactly ten minutes have passed, turn on the lights. Leave the candle burning, though.
- The leader asks, "How long do you think it has been since we lit the candle?"
- Family members give their estimates.
- The leader says, "It was ten minutes."
- "The voyage is now complete."

FEEDBACK: About this voyage, one father reported, "We had a great time. The combination of sitting on the floor and lighting the candle really made what is a familiar room in our house into a different place for us. The kids had an incredible attraction to the candlelight.

"We began making shadow-animals on the walls with our hands, something I hadn't done in years. The time seemed much longer than ten minutes. Most of us thought we had been there for a half-hour or so. We were a little sorry to go back to the ordinary lighting."

Another parent commented, "The kids' desire to blow out the candle became a major disruptive focus to the mood we were trying to establish. It would have been better to pick one child to blow out the candle at the end."

One eight-year-old boy said, "We built a fire in the fireplace—something we don't do very often. We turned off all the lights and sat and watched the fire for a long time. It felt like we were having an adventure right in our own living room."

FOLLOW-UP TO VOYAGE 1: In Voyage 1 we accomplished several important things:

- We set aside a physical place in the home for storytelling.

- We created a simple ritual (lighting the candle) to begin our voyages.
- We experienced the elasticity of time: We saw that our perception of times does not have to agree with what the hands on the clock say.
- We enjoyed simply being together, in the moment, without any fancy diversions.

Let's consider the importance of these points in our quest.

SPECIAL PLACE, FIRE, AND RITUAL

In our voyages in the imaginative world, it helps to have a physical spot that we know well to leave from and return to. Changing the lighting and the seating in the room makes this familiar place more special.

Throughout history, the fireplace or the woodstove was the focal point of the family's living space. A significant change took place when the fireplace was replaced by the furnace in the basement. The home lacked a hearthside and a center. In shifting from open flame to modern light sources, we have interrupted the natural balance of light and darkness in our lives. We satisfy this longing for fire in our simplest rituals—we light candles at birthdays, weddings, and funerals. We enjoy campfires in the summer and log fires in the fireplace in the winter. To have the light and warmth of fire in our lives is a basic human desire.

Stories and firelight go together. In his book *The Roots of Civilization*, anthropologist Alexander Marshak suggests that fire was the very first image humans were able to take into the imagination. Some forty-five thousand years ago, our distant ancestors looked into the fire at night and saw the flames with their physical eyes. Then they closed their eyes and discovered that they could also see the fire burning in their mind's eye. This recognition of our inner vision and an inner landscape was a great evolutionary leap for us. Marshak posits that this ability to see the world in measured, storylike images is an innately human trait that is passed along genetically from one generation to the next. In the voyages that follow, we will be drawing upon this ancestral, genetically encoded skill.

In addition to its power to evoke the imagination, fire has a magical ritual quality. Many anthropologists believe that the first human rituals involved the kindling and nurturing of this mysterious flaming thing that seems to have a life of its own. In lighting a candle, we enact thus a simple human ritual. In our secular culture, performing rituals is thought of as offbeat and weird. This stems from a misunderstanding of the true nature of ritual as a tool in everyday life. A ritual signals a shift to a new way of viewing the world. Our candle ritual is a clue to our minds and bodies that we are switching from outer to inner vision.

ELASTICITY OF TIME

It is refreshing to learn that clock time is not the only way of perceiving time in our lives. We can experience time subjectively as well. Storytelling is a skill that allows us to step out of linear, clock-reckoned time and into the realm of inner or subjective time. The storyteller evokes this experience of subjective time, not by chance or accident, but on purpose.

BEING IN THE MOMENT

What our kids most want from their parents is for us to be really present when we are with them. My own natural inclination is to do several things at once when I am spending time with my kids. Unless I pay close attention, though, I waste our time together by only half listening, half playing, half joining in their world. This is very unsatisfying for all of us. I have learned to use storytelling as a way of bringing me back into the moment so that I can be truly present when I am with my kids.

TELLING A STORY

Now that we have prepared the fire, established a ritual, and freed ourselves from the inflexibility of clock time, we are ready to begin telling our stories. The next voyage is probably the most important one in the book. In this voyage, we experience every facet of storytelling, from beginning to end. Keep in mind that we are not talking about anything new here. Rather we are reclaiming a natural ability that we already possess.

In Voyage 2 you will do the first of many guided visualizations in this book. You will follow the leader's instructions with eyes closed, seeing images in your mind's eye. Make the inner world as dark as possible. Simply close your eyes in the normal way. Note the density of the darkness. Some light probably seeps in. Use your facial muscles to close your eyelids tight. See what a difference this makes: it's much darker. Finally, cup your palms over your eyes, sealing out as much light as possible. Note how this is even darker still. This is a very tiring position, though. A thick cloth blindfold will also work well. I use a manufactured device, the Mindfold, in my workshops. It is made from light-weight foam and plastic, adjusts to fit any size head, and seals out light very well. Mindfolds can be ordered through the address in the Resources section at the back of the book.

Many people feel the voyages work best when they are lying down, completely relaxed. Try this posture during this voyage.

VOYAGE 2

The Storytelling Equation

TIME: 20 minutes

GOAL: To experience directly each phase of the storytelling process from creating to delivering the story; to gain an understanding of the storytelling/storylistening equation.

PREPARATION: Prepare the room. Settle the family, and light the candle. You need not note the time, but a watch will help you get a feel for the pauses and the pacing of the voyage.

INSTRUCTIONS:

- The leader says, "Let's sit quietly for a moment, with eyes open, and enjoy our fire." (30-second pause)
- "We are going to use the candle flame as a guide for a journey into the imagination. Let's begin by looking into the flame. This is a flame like the ones that generations of our ancestors looked into for hundreds of years. Like them, we can use the fire as a way of learning about storytelling. Continue to look into the candle flame." (30-second pause)
- "In a moment, I'm going to ask you to close your eyes and picture the candle flame in your imagination. Your eyes will be closed, but you will still see the flame. If you would be more comfortable lying down, you can do that now."
- "Let's close our eyes."
- "See the flame burning in your imagination. Using that flame as a guide, allow yourself to go back into memory. Locate a time when something happened with fire. Go back into your life and remember a time when something happened with fire." (30-second pause)
- "If you cannot locate something that happened with fire, that's OK. Any other memory from your past will work. If you find a fire memory, though, stick with that one."

- "Allow yourself to go back and daydream through that thing that happened. As you do this, your mind will automatically do something for you. It will automatically make a kind of movie of your daydream. It will be as though you have a movie camera in your head and are filming a movie and seeing it on a screen in your mind. So you will see the story not in words but in pictures. You don't have to do anything special. It will just happen naturally."
- "Take about a minute now to film that story and make your movie. You have plenty of time; don't rush through it. When you have completed your movie, store the film in memory, keep your eyes closed, and I will bring you back into the room." (60-second pause)
- "Finish up your movie. If you need more time, keep your eyes closed and raise your hand. We'll give you a few more moments to finish your film." (15-second pause if needed)
- "Complete your film and store it in memory. Now we are going to come back into the room. Keep your eyes closed, rub your hands together, rub your face, and, when you are ready, open your eyes and come back into the room." (10-second pause)
- "Now we begin the second part of the process. Using your movie as a guide, tell the story to a partner. Do not be concerned about the delivery of the story at this point. Simply put the movie into the projector, run the film, see it on the screen in your mind, and then describe what you see to your partner. We will give everyone a chance to listen and tell. Here's a tip: while you are telling your story, you want to look at two places at once. With your outer eyes, look at your partner; with your inner eyes, look at the movie on the screen in your imagination. Go ahead now and tell the story to your partner."
- "The voyage is now complete."

FEEDBACK: "I remembered a time when I was about eight years old and our kitchen curtains caught on fire," one parent noted. "I was surprised at how I was able to go back and reexperience everything so completely. It was not just visual: the smell of the burning curtains came back to me very clearly."

A nine-year-old girl said, "I remembered a time I roasted marshmallows around the fire with my dad. We had fun."

FOLLOW-UP TO VOYAGE 2: Congratulations! You have made a good start by telling a story resurrected from personal memory. Unconsciously, you have done several very sophisticated things in the course of telling your story. If we review them one by one, we can understand what makes storytelling work.

As the teller:

- We entered the inner world.
- We retrieved memory in the form of images.
- We captured these images by making a movie and storing the film in memory.
- We ran our movie on the inner screen and described the film to the listener.

As the listener, we heard the teller's words, turned on the inner projector, and saw a movie on our own inner screen, guided by the information the teller gave us.

THE INNER WORLD, MEMORIES, AND IMAGES

Dr. Joseph Murphy, author of *The Power of Your Subconscious Mind*, has shown that ninety percent of our mental life is subconscious during normal waking hours. If we imagine ourselves as icebergs, with ten percent above the surface of the water and ninety percent below, we might say that the world we enter through storytelling is below the surface of the water. In the most primal sense, a storyteller takes a journey into the inner world, brings back valuable information, and passes it along to others. When we close our eyes and go into the image of the candle flame, we are using the genetically coded ancestral memory of fire to take us back into that inner landscape. This is a land that is already familiar to us. We visit it each night in our dreams and during waking daydreams and reveries. Much of what scientists have learned from dream research can be applied to storytelling. Once we have made contact with the inner world, we can resurrect personal memories and childhood stories that were previously unavailable to us. We can use this same interior environment to create stories from scratch, and maybe even to tap into the genetic memory of our ancestors. It is vitally important for a storyteller to establish this basic connection with the lower ninety percent of the iceberg of consciousness. By doing this, you will be able to travel deep into your own inner world and bring back something of value to share with your family.

"FILMING" AND TELLING THE STORY

There is nothing original about my idea of "filming" or "dreaming up" the story. The Australian aborigines, who have lived and dreamed in one place for forty thousand years or more, call the other world "dreamtime" and believe our lives are all the dreams of some higher being—a very poetic interpretation of the process we just experienced.

In addition to its offering you a close connection with your inner world, there are several practical reasons why the movie camera technique is an attractive one for our work. It is not something we must learn; it is the way our minds work naturally. We don't think in words, we think in pictures. With all of our eagerness to have our children learn reading and writing skills, I think we sometimes forget what language really is. We somehow think the story resides in the words. That is simply not true. There are no stories in this book or in any other. There is nothing between these covers but ink and paper. The language is not the story; the words are simply a way of getting to the real story, the story that exists not in words but in pictures, in the mind.

The true source of a story is thus in the preverbal image in the mind. If we hold to the other idea, the idea that the story resides in the words, it's like going to a restaurant and eating the cardboard menu—but never eating any actual food. True storytelling means taking your listeners all the way back to the kitchen, where the real nutrition begins.

There is a long-standing tradition of storytelling that involves memorizing the words and delivering the story as a recitation. That technique only works, though, when the speaker has done the inner work well. I respect and honor the tradition of the old orators, but their method does not work well for most modern people.

When I tell a story, I take the film out of memory, put it in the projector, and view the movie on the inner screen. Then I find words to describe to the listener what I see. The beauty of this approach is that you don't need to worry about forgetting the words—there are no words. You don't need to worry about forgetting the plot—events simply follow each other naturally. Another advantage to this approach of mine is that you aren't tied down to any specific wording—you can allow the story to grow and change, improvising on the theme as a musician improvises on a familiar passage of music. If it is a good story, you can look into it year after year and always see more. I am still telling stories my father told me over thirty years ago. Those stories grow and change but still remain true to their original form. If I am telling a story I have told many times, there are certainly passages of dialogue or phrases I use again and again, but my reference points still remain in the pictures.

STORY-LISTENING

Amid all this talk about storytelling skills, it is important to remember that listening is an important skill too. A storyteller does not take the journey alone. The story must be a shared creation between teller and listener. We experienced this during Voyage 2. In that activity, we saw the whole process at work. Let's look at the machinery of that process. First, the teller brings the images up on a mental movie screen and translates these images into words for the listener. When the listeners hear the teller's words, their movie projectors kick in, and they begin to see the pictures on their movie screens.

What seems like a very simple process, then, is actually a very sophisticated one. If we made an equation of this process, it would look like this:

$$
\begin{aligned}
&\text{(Inner story } + \text{ teller)} \\
+\;&\text{language (verbal and nonverbal)} \\
+\;&\text{listener} \\
\hline
=\;&\text{a story in the listener's inner world}
\end{aligned}
$$

If any element of the equation is dropped out, the story will not work.

VOYAGE 3

The House Tour

TIME: 5 minutes

GOAL: To create vivid mental images.

PREPARATION: Prepare the room; have blindfolds and a wristwatch available. Light a candle.

INSTRUCTIONS:
- The leader says, "Let's close our eyes and sit quietly." (20-second pause)
- "See the front door of your house." (5-second pause)
- "Imagine now that you are taking a self-guided tour of

your house. As you enter through the door and go from room to room, feel free to stop and look at anything you please for as long as you please. You have plenty of time; there is no need to rush. Even though there is no one there with you, you may want to conduct the tour somewhat formally, stopping in each room and speaking for a few moments about the objects you see about the room itself."

- "I will give you about five minutes now to tour the house. Don't worry about the time; I'll watch it for you. When you have completed your tour, come back to the front door and I'll call you back."

- "Please open the door now and begin your tour." (5-minute pause)

- "If you need more time, keep your eyes closed and raise your hand. Let's take a few more minutes to make sure everyone has completed the tour and has returned to the front door." (60-second pause)

- "Exit your house and close the door behind you. Know that you can come back here anytime you want and stay for as long as you like. For now, though, we're coming back to this room. Keep your eyes closed, rub your hands together, rub your face, and, when you are ready, open your eyes and come back into the room."

- "The voyage is now complete."

FEEDBACK: One father said, "As a person who had trouble visualizing in the last voyage, I found this one very helpful. Strangely, instead of taking a tour through my present house, I went back to my childhood home. I could see everything pretty clearly, individual objects were very real to me. I was also surprised with the variety of feelings I associated with different parts of the house."

His daughter remarked, "I spent most of my time in the bedroom, looking at my own things. I was able to see them very well."

FOLLOW-UP TO VOYAGE 3: The ability to visualize is a learned skill for most of us. We can become better at it as time goes on. You may want to return to this familiar house tour later to see if you experience it with more clarity and as a way of gauging how sharp your inner vision is becoming. Along the way you may have noticed that, along with the visual components, you also get input from your other senses and form your emotions.

IN THE BODY

Let's take another voyage and concentrate on going even deeper into the story. This is my adaptation of an exercise that I learned from Barbara Freeman and Connie Regan-Blake. Scientific research has shown that the deepest involvement in guided visualization involves our going bodily into the movie, as opposed to seeing ourselves from afar. To read more about guided visualization, read Michael Bagley's *Using Imagery in Creative Problem Solving*.

VOYAGE 4

The Bike Ride

TIME: 10 minutes

GOAL: To experience the story on a more personal level by bringing it into the body; to recapture bodily sensations.

PREPARATION: Prepare the room; have blindfolds on hand; light the candle.

- The leader says, "Let's just sit quietly for a while and enjoy our fire." (Pause)
- "Now let's close our eyes." (Pause)
- "We are going to take a voyage back into memory. Go back into memory and remember the very first time you successfully rode a two-wheeled bicycle." (Pause)
- "If you cannot get that memory, that's OK. Pick something else that you learned how to do with your body. Maybe it was learning to swim or to play a musical instrument. Then think of the first time you did it really well. If you get the bike ride, though, stay with that, because that's a good one."
- "Using our movie camera trick, go back and make a film of that event. Remember that this time you won't see yourself from a distance but will experience the bike ride from inside your body, just as you did that day. You will look at things through your own eyes, just as you did when you were actually riding the bike."
- "I'll give you some time now to go back and make a film of the bike ride. When you have completed it, store it in memory and keep your eyes closed, and I will bring you back into the room."
- "If you need more time, keep your eyes closed and raise

your hand. That's fine. Let's take a few more moments to make sure you are all finished with your movies. Once you've completed yours, store it in memory and keep your eyes closed."

- "We're going to come back into the room now. Make sure your film is safely stored in memory and keep your eyes closed."

- "Tell your story to your partner."

- "The voyage is now complete."

FEEDBACK: A mother reported, "I was easily able to recall my first bike ride—it was sort of a rite of passage for me. My dad was running along beside me, holding on to the back of the bike seat. And then, suddenly, I couldn't see him anymore—and I realized I was riding alone!"

FOLLOW-UP TO VOYAGE 4: Telling stories is itself like riding a two-wheeler: it seems awkward at first, but once you find your balance, it becomes second nature.

Many who have taken this voyage comment that the bike ride is often a very vivid physical feeling. Authors like Jean Houston have written about the kinesthetic or "subtle" body. This is a body apart from our physical body that we can experience in a variety of ways. Houston gives the example of her uncle Paul, who lost a leg during World War II. When she was a girl, her uncle would ask her to scratch his toe. Even though he didn't have a physical toe anymore, his kinesthetic toe would still get itchy at times. In medical circles, this phenomenon is called the "phantom limb." If you'd like to have a clear experience of leaping in and out of your physical body with your kinesthetic body, consult Houston's book *The Possible Human*.

My own feeling is that it is the kinesthetic body that storytellers use when telling a story like the one about the bike ride. This feeling of being physically immersed in the story we are telling is akin to the vividness of dreams in which we are running, falling, or moving in other ways.

The physical closeness to the story we are telling allows us to feel as well as see the action taking place in the inner world. Remember what I said before about Bagley's research on the intensity of dream experience.

Dreams in which we are physically in our bodies tend to be more intense than ones in which we are observing ourselves from afar. The same is true for our stories.

SUMMARY

In Voyages 1–4, we learned to translate a personal memory into a story. This same technique, with a few modifications, will work for learning and telling any story, regardless of its source. You can use this technique to learn stories from books or records or from other people. You can use it to learn poetry or even to create your own stories. We'll deal with the specifics of these applications in chapter 3, "Bringing the Story to Life."

Throughout the rest of the book you will be making voyages in essentially the same way you did in this chapter. Note that you don't need the room preparation and the candle to make these voyages work. I encourage you to take these stories with you wherever you go. Experiment with telling stories in the car, for example. Do set aside some time to tell stories in the quiet of the home, by candlelight, though.

Don't hesitate to tell the stories as they come to you. If these voyages have shaken loose some additional memories, be sure to tell them. The best way to learn to tell stories is simply to tell them. Don't forget to listen to your children's stories as well. Once you start telling stories, your children will follow your lead.

This has been the most important chapter in the book. We have made important progress, laying a firm foundation for the voyages ahead. Once we get the inner skills working properly, we can begin with outer tools. When you are ready, move ahead to the skills with which you will communicate your story.

CHAPTER 2

Venturing Out

Learning the Language of Voice, Motion, and Gesture

In this chapter, we will:

- Make an inventory of the storyteller's "outer tools."
- Review the uses of each tool, with exercises to sharpen your senses.
- Give general guidelines for using your outer tools effectively.
- Tell a story with special attention to how using your outer tools can bring the story to life.

Now that we have got the inner tools working properly, let's focus on the outer tools of the storyteller—the means by which the teller communicates the story to the listener. Remember the storytelling equation; it is important that both the inner and outer tools work together. Obviously, a story is of no interest if you cannot communicate it to the listener. The reverse is also true: if you haven't done your inner work, even the most skillful use of your outer tools will be to no avail. The skillful storyteller abides in both worlds at once. In this chapter we will work on blending these new skills so that the inner and outer tools work in harmony. Of course, the best way to use your inner and outer tools is not simply to read about them but to tell stories and listen to the stories of others. If you know a skillful storyteller whom you can observe, he or she can model how the outer tools are used, and you can adapt what you like and reject what you don't like.

Let's begin with an inventory of the outer tools at our disposal. They fall into two broad categories: verbal tools (words and sounds we make with our voices) and nonverbal tools (facial expressions, eye contact, gestures, and body language).

VERBAL TOOLS: THE VOICE

You don't need a voice to tell a story. Dance can tell a story; so can mime or silent theater. Since we are working with storytelling primarily as a spoken art, though, let's begin with the use of voice.

The quality of the sound of the storyteller's voice is crucial. Tribal cultures all over the world have recognized this for thousands of years.

The overtone chants of the Tibetan monks, the Gregorian chants of the Roman Catholic monks, and the drum-accompanied chants of the Lakota Sioux all spring from a common idea: sound charges us, heals us, releases endorphins in the brain. Western science is rediscovering the healing qualities of sound. Some sounds charge our energies, and some sounds discharge them. We receive sound not through our ears alone, but with all of our skin. Our skin tells the story to the whole body. Scientists are only now beginning to understand the subtleties of sound. (See the Resources section for some new research on the uses of sound.)

You don't need to understand the intricacies of sonic research in order to experience the effects sound has upon us. As the saying goes, "Understanding is the booby prize." The best way I know to feel the effect of sound on the body uses the help of the Hindu chakra system. The ancient Hindus identified seven centers of subtle, powerful energy in the body, called chakras. Each chakra is associated with a certain note on the musical scale and with a certain syllable that activates and charges it. If you find this idea strange, remember that our journey can take us to many unusual places; that's the path of the adventurer. The exercise you will practice in Voyage 5 is one that I learned from Jim Swan, who based it on work done by the musician Steven Halpern.

VOYAGE 5

Sounding the Notes of the Body

TIME: 10 minutes

GOAL: To feel the physical effects that different sounds have on our bodies.

PREPARATION: Prepare the room, seat the family, light the candle. No blindfolds are needed. You will need a musical instrument: a piano, a guitar, a pitch pipe—any device that can sound out the notes from middle C up the scale to B.

• Light the candle.

• "Let's sit quietly and enjoy the flame from our candle."

- "We are going to have some fun now, as we notice how different sounds feel in our bodies. To do this, we are going to use a system from India called sounding the chakras (pronounced *chock*-ruhz). The chakras are the seven energy centers in the body. For each chakra I will give you a note and a sound to make. Then we will take a breath, I will give you the note, and we will make the sound. Just let your breath flow out naturally."

- "The first chakra is located at the base of the spine. This is the source of power and pleasure, and it links us to the earth. The note is C. The sound we make is LOM (pronounced *loam*). Let's try it. Place your attention at the base of the spine."

- Strike the note; have everyone sing in unison, "LOMMMMMM . . ."

- "Notice how the sound feels in each part of your body as we sing it."

- The second chakra is located just below the navel. This is the center of emotions and creativity. The note is D. The sound is VOM (pronounced *voam*). Direct your attention to the navel. Let's try it."

- Strike the note; have everyone sing in unison, "VOMMMMMM . . ."

- The next chakra is located at the stomach. This chakra is related to assertiveness, order, and structure. The note is E. The sound is ROM (*roam*). Focus your attention on the upper stomach area. Let's do it."

- Strike the note; have everyone sing in unison, "ROMMMMMM . . ."

- "The fourth chakra is at the heart and is related to compassion and generosity. The note is F. The sound is AUM (*aum*). Place your attention in the heart area. Let's sing it."

- Strike the note and sing, "AUMMMMMM . . ."

- "Good. The next chakra is in the throat area. It has to do with courage. The note is G. the sound is HOM (*home*). Our attention is in the throat now. Let's try it."

- Strike the note and sing, "HOMMMMMM . . ."

- "Sounds great. The sixth chakra is in the center of the forehead, the place of knowing rapture. The note is A. The sound is OM (*om*). Focus on the center of the forehead. Let's do it."

- Strike the note and sing, "OMMMMMM . . ."
- "Good. The last chakra is located just above the head and has to do with the divine. The note is B. The sound is OM, sung in the key of B. Direct your attention to the space above your head. Let's sing it."
- Strike the note and sing, "OMMMMMM . . ."
- "Let's sit quietly now for a few moments before we talk about our experience."
- "The voyage is now complete."

FEEDBACK: "I like the OM sound," a girl of eleven said. "It reminded me of the sound whales make when they are swimming in the ocean."

A mother said, "I was surprised at how energized I felt by the singing. I closed my eyes and clearly felt the sounds instead of just hearing them. I also felt a little sad when I realized that our family very rarely sings together. I rarely hear my children's voices mixed with mine the way they were in this voyage. When I was a girl, we used to sing around the piano every evening after dinner. I think I'll start to do that with my own family."

FOLLOW-UP TO VOYAGE 5: I, too, am always surprised at how awakened and alive I feel when I do this exercise. Since I first discovered this, I have looked for other sounds that give the same result. Gregorian chants, sung by the Franciscan Friars in France, work well for me. When I am on a long drive, or just working at my desk at home, I play tapes of these sounds to keep awake and energized. I also enjoy drum, flute, and harp music. All of these are charging sounds for me. Do some exploring on your own to find out which sounds charge you. Be aware, though, that listening to a recording of sounds can never equal the intense physical effect of hearing them live.

Perhaps the greatest benefit that our sons and daughters receive from story-listening, besides the content of the story, is the sound of their parent's voice. When you read a story to your child, notice how your tone changes from that of your everyday voice. This different sound is an invitation to listen in a different way—to listen with the heart. A very good model of a storyteller's voice is that of Fred Rogers, the creator of the TV show "Mister Rogers' Neighborhood." Rogers looks into the camera as if looking deep into a child's eyes, and speaks from the heart to his listeners. He never addresses youngsters in a cutesy or patronizing way but treats them with gentleness and respect.

FINDING YOUR VOICE

Most of us go through our lives misusing our vocal equipment, so we never experience our full vocal abilities. I found this out the hard way. During my first year of full-time storytelling I was dogged by sore throats, colds, and mouth ulcers. I knew that if I was going to stay in this profession—indeed, if I was going to keep my voice at all—I would have to find a voice teacher. In a year of lessons I learned a tremendous amount about the proper use of my voice. Not only did my health problems clear up, but I also gained a new voice, one that is stronger and more resilient, and more interesting to listen to. Voyage 6 incorporates a few things I learned about the proper use of the voice.

Great voices are born. It is a rare person, though, who actually uses his or her voice to the best advantage. We can all work to make our voices stronger and more interesting. Here are three principles of proper use of the instrument. Being aware of these techniques can help you make better use of your voice.

BREATHING. Words are breath. Most of us breathe shallowly into the upper chest. We can put more gas in the tank if we use a simple technique called breathing from the diaphragm.

Here's how it works:

- Stand normally, with one hand on your stomach.
- Take a deep breath into the upper chest and, as you let it out, say, "OHHHHHH . . ." Keep the breath going as long as you can.
- Now try breathing consciously from the diaphragm. As you breathe in, make the hand on your stomach go out. Practice that a few times.
- Now take a breath into your stomach or diaphragm, and let it out, saying, "OHHHHHH . . ."
- Feel the difference? You used more air, so you had a

VOYAGE 6

*Using
Your Vocal
Instrument*

greater vocal capacity. The deeper breath gives your words more power and a more pleasing sound.

RELAXING THE VOCAL CORDS. When my teacher asked me to hum scales, he would say, "Make the sounds with your vocal cords relaxed." I was surprised. I had thought I made sounds by tensing my vocal cords. On the contrary, my teacher explained, if my throat was not completely relaxed, I could hurt my voice and tire myself out needlessly.

Here's a trick to help you relax the throat area:

- Stand normally and hum: "HUMMMMMM . . ."
- Use your index finger and thumb to lightly pinch the wattle of skin underneath your chin. Notice any muscle tension there. Make a conscious effort to relax the area, and try humming now with the throat muscles relaxed.
- Hum several times. Try to produce a sound with complete freedom from tension in the throat.
- Try singing, "MA, MA, MA, MA, MAAAAAA . . . ," going up the scale. Keep the throat relaxed.

SINGING FROM THE HEAD. "But if my vocal cords are relaxed," I asked my teacher, "How am I going to make the sounds?"

"With your head," he answered. My teacher explained that the voice sound is generated by the air passing over the vocal cords, but the sound gains resonance and volume in the cranium, especially in the area called the mask, or sinus area, of the eyes, nose, and forehead.

To experience mask singing, try this:

- Using your thumb and forefinger, lightly pinch the skin at the bridge of your nose.
- Say, "HMMMMMM . . ."
- Feel the physical sense of vibration the sound makes as it moves around your nasal area. You may have to move your fingers around a bit to feel this.
- Now, this time when you say, "HMMMMMM . . . ," make a conscious effort to place the sound in your nose and in your sinus cavity. Feel it resonate there.
- Now try saying, "Me? Who, me?" Feel those words resonate in your face and forehead area. Don't force the sound, finesse it. Let it float up there easily.
- Experiment with this new vocal sound by singing, "ME, ME, ME, ME, MEEEEEE . . . ," going up the scale. Then try

"MA, MA, MA, MA, MAAAAAA . . . ," letting the last note resonate as long as possible.

- Pay attention now to your new voice—not just the sound of it, but the physical feel of the voice in your body. For most of us, this will be a very different way of using our voices.
- Try speaking a few lines from the beginning of a story and notice how your voice is working. As you speak, remember to make use of all three of these elements: the diaphragm breathing, the relaxed throat, and the resonance in the head.

TYPES OF VOICES AND VOCAL SOUNDS

The storyteller's voice can be used in four ways:

- Narrator's voice
- Character voices
- Singing voice
- Sound effects

Narrator's Voice

It's important to know who is telling the story. Most of the stories we tell have a narrator. In storytelling, though, the teller does all the characters' voices, including that of the narrator. Obviously, if you are telling a story about a bike ride when you were a kid, you are the narrator—but you are also a character. If you are telling a fairy tale, you have more distance from the subject, and your narrator will be relatively low-keyed. Beware of your handling of the narrator's voice so that it balances with the other voices in the story.

Character Voices

Most stories consist of a pattern of dialogue and action. Your characters will probably have speaking parts. To help the listener know who is speaking, you can use phrases like "he said," or "she said," or "the witch screamed." A more effective way to differentiate the speakers is to give each character a distinctive voice.

If you feel comfortable doing character voices, use them. They add greatly to the fun of telling stories. Build yourself a repertoire of characters. Start out with the stereotypes: the evil witch, the shy princess, the brave hero—but don't stop there. While there is a grain of truth in all stereotypes, it is also true that not all old women are evil witches, and princesses are not all necessarily shy. In the story "Rapunzel," for instance, the witch teaches Rapunzel something valuable: Rapunzel discovers her own hidden reserves of strength.

A great way to learn character voices is to listen to the radio and mimic the voices you hear. Be outrageous. From the brash banter of the wholesale carpet salesman to the smooth-as-silk murmurs of the classical music concert host, the radio offers a banquet for the ear. Also note that in doing character voices, the facial expression and the posture of the character will help you to find the voice.

Singing

Singing adds a welcome texture to a spoken story. In many cultural traditions there is no distinction between a storyteller, a poet, and a singer. Many old stories were sung and were accompanied by a drum or a harp.

There are many stories that have songs embedded in them as an integral part of their plot. An example is the Grimms' fairy tale "The Juniper Tree," in which a bird sings a song telling about a boy who is buried beneath a juniper tree. When my family makes up stories around our house, we often throw in an original song to keep the plot moving along. In its purest form, singing is at the heart of the storyteller's art.

Sound Effects

The sounds of popping corks, tramping feet, and whistling birds added life to old-time radio dramas. Sound effects can do the same for our stories. Every kid has developed a repertoire of these sounds. A word of caution, though: use these devices sparingly. Sounds effects can be so engaging that they draw attention away from the forward progress of the story.

The best source I know for learning these sounds is Frederick R. Newman's *Mouthsounds* book and record, which give step-by-step instructions for creating animal calls, household sounds, and even rude body noises. (See the Resources section.)

NONVERBAL TOOLS

Facial Expressions

The face of the storyteller is like the canvas of the painter. Through facial expression we can portray every feeling from righteousness to lust, and we can evoke these feelings in our listeners. Just as all characters have their own voices, they also have their own facial expressions.

I don't usually advise rehearsing stories in front of a mirror; it makes the storyteller too self-conscious. Rather, you want to lose yourself in the story. However, the mirror can be a great tool when you are developing characters. I like to check my facial expressions in the mirror before I put the character into a story. Try it for yourself: make yourself as grotesque as possible. Make yourself frightened. Make yourself noble. Have fun with your face.

Eye Contact

We grip and release our listeners with our eyes. The eyes are indeed windows of the soul. We all know how disconcerting it is to talk to someone who won't look us in the eye.

When I tell a story, I look directly at my listeners. I do not look off into the distance unless I am using my glance to indicate the location of something or unless some specific character is looking away. This is one of the essential differences between theater and storytelling. In the theater, the story takes place on the stage. In storytelling, it takes place in the mind of the listener. Even in this era of sophisticated electronic entertainment contraptions, there is still something quite arresting about looking into the eyes of another person and hearing a story told from the heart.

Of course, if you are telling to several people, you will need to roam about with your glance, making eye contact with a different listener every few seconds. Let your listeners know that you see them.

Even though it lasts only one minute, Voyage 7 is the most difficult one in the book. The benefits are tremendous. I first experienced this in Werner Erhard's work, and it has radically changed my ability to "face" other people.

TIME: 1 minute

GOAL: To remove the false, "pasted-on" mask that we normally wear, and reveal our true face; to confront our fear and discomfort about making eye contact with others.

PREPARATION: Prepare the room. You will need to work with a partner for this one. You will also need a wristwatch with a sweep second hand.

VOYAGE 7

Taking Off the Mask

INSTRUCTIONS:
- Seat partners across from each other in chairs or on the floor, with a few feet in between.
- "Look into your partner's face for sixty seconds, doing your best to maintain eye contact the whole time."
- "Observe your reaction closely."
- "The voyage is now complete."

FEEDBACK: "This exercise was very difficult for me to do," one woman confessed. "My face at first felt hard and strained, but after a while my muscles gave up and gave in. I wiped the phony smile off my face and simply looked. I was aware of how frightened I was to make extended eye contact with another person, even my husband."

"I was laughing so much I couldn't do it at first, but then I saw that my laughter was just covering up my discomfort," another parent said. "When I continued to look into my son's eyes, I finally saw that it was all right and that it was safe to just let my face be exactly as it was. I realized how much energy I expend trying to put on a false face."

FOLLOW-UP TO VOYAGE 7: This is a difficult exercise. It requires hanging in there long enough for the mask to fall off. We all wear a public mask, even in front of our family. Even as we search for our true voice, we must also search for a glimpse of our true face, the face that lies behind the mask.

As the poet W. B. Yeats said, "I want to wear the face I wore before the world was made."

That is the storyteller's face, the face that simply is. It is a face that can assume the masks of the characters. The vitality of expression, though, must come from this unmasked face underneath. If you want to see some unmasked faces, look at your young children. They are just what they are. In this regard, our children are our greatest teachers.

The psychologist Marion Woodman puts it this way: "If we have lived behind a mask all our lives, sooner or later—if we are lucky—that mask will be smashed. . . . Perhaps we will look into the terrified eyes of our own tiny child, that child who has never known love and who now beseeches us to respond." The inner child, the one that lives in the psyche, can also be a great teacher for us. For a comprehensive discussion of this concept, see *Reclaiming the Inner Child*, edited by Jeremiah Abrams.

The freedom to take on parts and play roles comes from a strong link to your own true face.

GESTURES AND BODY LANGUAGE

Just as we seek to express ourselves with our true voice and our true face, we also want to move our body freely, entering the story physically, unencumbered by layers of societally induced armor plating.

VOYAGE 8

Taking Off the Armor

TIME: 1 minute

GOAL: To free the body from the protective emotional armor it habitually wears so that our gestures and body movements are free and spontaneous, true reflections of our story.

PREPARATION: Prepare the room. You need a partner and a wristwatch.

INSTRUCTIONS:

- "Stand normally, facing your partner, with a few feet in between."
- "Look silently at your partner, paying special attention to how your stance feels, for sixty seconds."
- "The voyage is now complete."

FEEDBACK: "This was very awkward for me," one mother noted. "I stood with my arms crossed for a while, but my body seemed very rigid, so I dropped my hands to my sides and tried to stand more naturally. I finally relaxed enough to see how rigidly I ordinarily stand."

FOLLOW-UP TO VOYAGE 8: We all have adopted protective armoring postures in our own lives. We develop these defenses as we are growing up, as we are getting our "act" together. They don't help us, though, when it comes time to tell stories. Just as a rigid face prevents the story from shining through us, the body covered with protective armor is also a poor storytelling tool. When we tell stories, we are unmasking, disarming ourselves.

I learned a technique that helps me during a mime workshop with my friend Bill Mettler. Bill taught me to stand in a neutral position, feet apart, relaxed and open. Find what works for you and try it with your partner. Every story can begin and end in this position.

Your listeners are your mirrors. If you are uptight and strained, they will be too.

TIPS ON USING YOUR TOOLS

Keep It Simple

The storyteller need not describe everything in infinite detail. That would leave nothing for the listener to do. The art of storytelling is not so much about what you include as it is about what you leave out. The storyteller suggests, then lets the listener fill in the blanks. Economy is good sense, and a virtue in itself. Better to tell a simple tale well than a complex tale poorly.

Easy Does It

Slow down. Most stories improve by telling them at about half speed. The storyteller's time moves at a different rate than does time in everyday life—sometimes faster, but usually slower. Storytelling is auditory, and both the ear and the mouth need time to savor the words. While there are some parts of stories that call for a quicker pace, use this fast-forward speech sparingly. If you start out at ninety miles an hour, where can you go from there?

Slowing down also lets silence come into your tale. Silence is to the storyteller as the darkness of the night sky is to a fireworks expert. If there were no darkness, the fireworks would not be nearly so spectacular. Let the silence seep in around your words, and you will find yourself working with it almost like a singer working with an accompanist. As Bach once said, "Music is playing the space between the notes." A similar observation could be made for storytelling.

Travel in Style

We all have a certain style of doing things. The judgment that guides how we use our storytelling tools is based on style. There are no rules about style. What works, works. Listen to other tellers, and emulate what you admire in their styles in order to develop your own style. The central element of style is poise, which is grace under pressure.

Tricks of the Trade

Commit the first three lines and the last line of your story to memory. When telling a prepared tale, get off to a good, clean start and have a good, strong ending. Memorizing these lines is your insurance against nervousness and disorganized thinking. Delivering the first three lines by rote gives the movie camera time to kick in so that you can ride out the rest of the story, freelancing with the images on the inner screen. A well-thought-out ending line likewise will bring closure to the story.

When developing characters, work with contrasts. In folktales, we very rarely encounter more than two people speaking at once. We don't want the listeners to become confused and lose the flow of the story because they can't identify who is talking. If your characters speak in distinctive voices, listeners can easily follow their conversations.

Make use of audience participation, sound effects, and bits of stagecraft as they occur to you. Keep in mind, though, that the forward motion of the story is the most important part of story-telling. Use your judgment to avoid anything that derails that progress.

STEP BY STEP THROUGH A STORY

Let's walk our way through a folktale, paying special attention to how we can use our outer tools to bring the story to life. The suggestions here are models for the use of the tools we have discussed.

This is a story I heard when I was a boy and have been telling ever since. It comes from James Mooney's *Myths of the Cherokee*. Get the feel of the story first by reading it aloud.

Turtle and the Wolves

One day Possum was up in a tree, picking persimmons— which are a sticky fruit—and throwing them down to Turtle. This was in the days when all the animals could talk and the turtle's shell was completely smooth and shining like a mirror.

Every time Possum would toss down one of those persimmons, Turtle would open his mouth and [*ump*] swallow one of those persimmons.

It was while that was going on that a great big wolf came out of the woods. He sat down next to Turtle, and every time Possum would toss down one of those persimmons, Wolf would open his greedy jaws and [*ump*] swallow one of them.

Turtle didn't like that. He turned to Possum and said, "Throw him down a really big one." Then he winked.

Possum picked a great big sticky persimmon and threw it right down to Wolf. Wolf opened his jaws and [*ump*] swallowed that persimmon. Or tried to swallow it, because he got it stuck in his throat, and he fell over with his feet sticking up in the air.

Turtle said, "That will teach those wolves to fool with me." And he walked off.

There was Wolf, lying under that persimmon tree with his feet up in the air, when a pack of his fellow wolves came running through that clearing. They saw that their friend was in trouble. They slapped him on the back, and Wolf coughed up that persimmon.

Once the wolf had caught his breath, he became furious.

"How humiliating," he growled, "to have my fellow wolves save me from a turtle. I'm gonna get that turtle and teach him a lesson."

Well, it didn't take Wolf long to catch up with Turtle. He picked him up by the shell and carried him all the way back to the wolves' den, where the other wolves had a big fire going under a pot of boiling water.

Wolf put Turtle down on the ground. Turtle poked his head out of his shell and looked around.

"Now listen here, Turtle," Wolf said. "You see that big pot of water over there on the fire? I'm gonna take you and throw you into that pot and boil you to make some turtle soup for me and my fellow wolves."

The turtle said, "Oh, yeah? Well I'll tell ya what: You toss me into that pot, I'm just gonna kick it to pieces."

"Whoooooo!" Wolf said. "I didn't think of that! Well, all right, I'll throw you in the fire and roast you up!"

"Oh, yeah?" Turtle said. "You throw me in that fire, I'm just gonna roll all around with my shell and stamp every bit of it out."

"Whoooooo!" Wolf said. "I didn't think of that! Well, all right, I don't even care about eating you. I'll just take you and throw you into that river!"

Now you and I know that the turtle's a good swimmer, but the wolf didn't know that.

"Well," Turtle said, "you could throw me in that pot, you could throw me in that fire, but whatever you do, don't throw me in that river!"

"That's exactly what I'm gonna do," Wolf said, and he

picked that turtle up and threw him into the river. Turtle hit the water and swam away, laughing.

That should be the end of the story, except for one thing: just before he went into the water, Turtle struck a great big rock in the center of the river, and his shell cracked into a dozen tiny pieces.

When Turtle crawled out onto the bank on the other side, he was laughing. But then he looked back and saw that his beautiful shell that he was so proud of had been destroyed.

Turtle lay down in the sun and let the sun shine on him and heal him up. But it didn't heal him completely. And to this day, if you look at a turtle's shell, you can still see those cracks he got from hitting that big old rock in the center of the river.

While this story is still fresh in your mind, close your eyes and make a film clip of it, just as you did with your personal-experience stories. Don't skip this step of seeing the story enacted in your inner world. Even though we will be focusing on using outer tools here, the vitality of your telling, as always, will depend upon your inner vision of the story.

When you tell this story, pay special attention to the use of your outer tools. Here are a few examples of how the tools we discussed can be used to make this story come alive.

Gesture

We are given an opportunity early in the story to use gesture as a way of eliciting audience participation in the story. When the possum first tosses the persimmon down to the turtle, I like to use both of my hands, held in front of my face, to mime the turtle's mouth opening for the persimmon. I start with my hands open, and when the possum throws down the persimmon, I make the sound effect—"*ump!*"—and clap my hands shut. Then I ask my listeners, "Do you want to help me do that? Get your jaws up there." They hold their hands up, and I give them an opportunity to run through the line with me: "Every time that possum would throw down one of those persimmons, that turtle would open his mouth and—all together, now—*ump!*" This is usually all the cue they need to play their part correctly through the remainder of the story. Part of the fun of this type of story is when the kids catch on to the repetition and can anticipate when their part is coming up.

An opportunity for full body movement comes up when the

wolf chokes and falls over with his feet up in the air. I sometimes roll over on my back with my legs held rigid. A less dramatic approach is to use your fingers to indicate the wolf's position.

Use gestures throughout the story to indicate the spatial relationship of the story setting. For instance, in the scene outside the wolves' den, it's important to have a clear idea of where things are. While your listeners are picturing the story in their minds, they are also taking cues from your use of space in the room. If you don't keep the pot and the fire in the same place, regardless of how your characters move about, you are going to confuse your listeners. You can indicate the position of the pot by directing your gestures and gaze to that spot. By the same token, when your characters are turning to face each other when they speak, keep the spatial relationships consistent.

Characterizations

Using character voices can be great fun in a story like this. Here we can contrast the slow, unflappable composure of the turtle with the high-strung, barely contained fury of the wolf. I get into the position of the turtle by bending forward and sticking my neck out, looking around with my mouth moving slowly and laconically, almost as if I were chewing tobacco. I give plenty of chews and pauses between the words and let the lines trail out the way Jimmy Stewart used to in the old black-and-white movies.

For the wolf, I assume an upright, uptight position and flail around a lot. Let's look at the wolf's first spoken line: "How humiliating to have my fellow wolves save me from a turtle."

Here I use a glowering body posture, an infuriated facial expression, and a voice like sandpaper, speaking in a tone that hungers for revenge. The wolf can really play the buffoon here, depending upon how you handle his lines. For instance, when the turtle first challenges the wolf's threat to throw him in the pot and cook him, the wolf says, "Whooooooo! I didn't think of that. Well, all right, I'll throw you in the fire and roast you up!"

There are a lot of ways the wolf can deliver this line. Here's one possibility: "Whooooooo!" (The wolf is shocked at the turtle's courage.) "I didn't think of that." (He can address this comment to the listeners. The turtle has taken the wind out of his sails for the moment.) "Well, all right"—he's regaining his balance now—"I'll throw you in the fire and roast you up!" (He delivers this line with relish, proud of himself for doing some quick thinking.)

Notice that you must take on four roles in this story—the possum, the turtle, the wolf, and the narrator.

The narrator gets the story off to a good start and gives a good, strong ending. The narrator is also present to give vital information. For instance, early in the story the narrator explains in a quick aside that a persimmon is a sticky fruit. Some kids may not know what a persimmon is. "This was in the days when a turtle's shell was smooth and shining like a mirror" is another aside, delivered in a kind of conspiratorial voice, asking the listener to accept that this is one of the "givens" of the story.

Finally, the narrator could use a real turtle shell as a prop, actually showing the cracks on the shell. Try this, and you'll find that your children will never forget the mythological "reason" for the cracks on the turtle's shell.

These are only a few of the ways you can use your outer tools to spice up the story. Remember that there is no "right" way to do this. Each teller must find the interpretation that suits him or her. You should also feel free to experiment with different shades of meaning each time you tell a story, improvising on a familiar theme, as a jazz musician does.

A story, like a person or a planet, is a whole system. As you tell the story again and again, it will evolve and eventually come together in your telling so that you won't be conscious of its individual elements any more than you are conscious of the beating of your heart or the workings of the cells of your body. In order to get to that point, you should tell a carefully prepared story as many times as you can, paying particular attention to the use of your outer tools. The key to all spontaneity is careful preparation. Once you have mastered the details of the telling of the story, you will free yourself to fly with it.

A MORE COMPLEX STORY

I adapted the following story from one I read in Jack Maguire's *Creative Storytelling*. Maguire notes that this story comes to us from Paddy John Halloran, an old-time Irish storyteller. Read the story aloud. Then dream it up on your inner screen. Then tell it, paying special attention to the use of your outer tools.

Note the introduction of another audience participation gambit here: the call and response. You ask, "Did she do a good job?" Your listeners answer, "No!" You confirm it, "No." Listeners' responses are in parentheses.

Eileen Aroon

Long ago there lived a girl named Eileen Aroon. She was the laziest girl in all of Ireland. She was so lazy, her mother couldn't get her to do anything around the house.

Her mother said, "Eileen, if you don't learn to do a few things around the house, you're never going to have a house of your own, you're never going to have a husband of your own, you're never going to have kids of your own—"

"Oh, I'm not going to have to worry about any of that," Eileen said. "I'm going to marry a prince on a white horse in shining armor; I'm going to live in a castle and have servants do all my work."

"Eileen, that's not going to happen! You are going to learn to do a few things around this house today. You see that pot of soup over there on the fire? Go over and stir it and see that it doesn't boil over. I'm going out to get some firewood. I'll be right back."

"Oh, all right," Eileen said. She walked over and started to stir the pot of soup.

Did she do a good job?

(No)

No, she didn't.

She was staring off into space, daydreaming about the prince, when her mother came in with a load of firewood. Her mother saw that the pot had boiled over and had put out the fire, and Eileen hadn't even noticed.

"Ooooooh, you bad girl." She grabbed Eileen by the ear and dragged her out into the front yard. She bent over her and was just about to give Eileen a good whack on the bottom when she looked up and . . . there, coming down the road, riding on a white horse, wearing shining armor—who was it?

(The prince)

The prince!

He said, "Madame, what are you doing with this beautiful young woman?"

Eileen's mother said, "Ooooooh! I should tell you about this beautiful young woman! She is the laziest—"

Eileen's mother saw that the girl and the prince were looking at each other like two puppies in love.

"I mean, she is the hardest-working girl in all of Ireland. I have to beat her to keep her from working." Is she telling the truth?

(No)

No.

The prince said, "I'd love to marry a girl like that."

Eileen said, "I'll get my things."

So she went inside, got her few little things, then hopped on the back of the prince's horse. "Ta-ta, Ma."

Off they went to the castle.

The first thing the prince did was introduce Eileen to his own mother.

His mother would be the queen, wouldn't she?

(Yes)

Yes, she was the queen.

The queen looked at Eileen and said, "So, you're the hardest-working girl in all of Ireland. If you are, you won't have any trouble doing this—come with me, my dear."

The queen took her up into a room at the top of a tall stone tower. When they walked into the room, all Eileen could see was—

Does everybody know what wool is?

(Yes)

All she could see was a big pile of wool on the floor. And then Eileen looked around—

Does everyone know what a spinning wheel is?

(Yes)

In the corner of the room sat a spinning wheel.

"If you're really the hardest-working girl in all of Ireland, you won't have any trouble taking all this wool and spinning it up into thread. By the way, my dear, if it's not done by sundown tonight, it will be the worse for you!"

The queen slammed the door. Eileen sat down and began to cry.

"What am I going to do? I should have listened to my mother. She wanted to teach me about spinning wheels. I didn't want to learn. What am I going to do?"

Just then, Eileen heard a little voice beside her. The voice said, "I could help you."

The girl looked up, and there, standing in the corner of the room, was a little green gnome.

Does everybody here know what a gnome is?

(Yes)

He was a little gnome about three feet high. He said again, "I could help you."

"Oh, you could help me?"

"Yes, but you'd have to promise to do something for me."

"All right, what do you want?"

"You'd have to promise to invite me to your wedding."

"What? You mean you're going to do all this work for me, you're going to save me, and all I have to do is invite you to my wedding?"

"Yes."

The green gnome sat down at the spinning wheel.

Did he know about spinning wheels?

(Yes)

He started to work the—what do you call that thing?

(Pedal)

He started to work the pedal. He spun all the wool into thread. He worked that whole day. He was just finishing up the last bit as the sun was dipping down in the sky, when he and Eileen heard the queen's heavy footsteps coming up the stairway.

The green gnome said, "I've got to go!" He put his hand up over his head and—*whoosh*—he disappeared in a puff of green smoke.

The queen came in and said, "Well, I knew you'd never be able to—Eileen! You did it! It would have taken a dozen girls three days to do that job. How did you do it?"

Eileen looked sheepishly toward the queen. "Oh, that? I finished that job hours ago."

Is she telling the truth?

(No)

No.

The queen smiled. "Maybe you really are the hardest-working girl in all of Ireland. You can come to dinner now."

Was the queen satisfied?

(No)

No.

The next morning after breakfast, the queen said, "You did that job so well yesterday, I've got another job for you. Come with me, my dear."

She took Eileen up in the tower. There was the thread from the day before, and in the corner of the room, there stood a loom.

Does everybody know what a loom is?

(Yes)

The queen said, "You did so well with that thread, I want you to weave it up into cloth on this loom. By the way, dear, if it's not done by sundown tonight, it'll be the worse for you!" And she slammed the door.

Eileen sat down and began to cry. "Oh, no, what am I going to do? My mother was right. She wanted to teach me about looms. I didn't want to learn."

Just then Eileen heard a little voice beside her. It said, "I can help you."

She looked up, and there was that little green gnome.

"Oh, could you help me?"

"Yes, but you'd have to promise to do something for me."

"What?"

"You'd have to promise to invite me to your wedding."

"But I already said I'd do that. Is that all you want?"

"Yes."

"All right, go to it!"

The green gnome sat down at the loom. Did he know about looms?

(Yes)

Yes.

He worked the loom all that day and wove up a beautiful bolt of cloth. He was just tying off the last knot as the sun was dipping down in the sky when they heard the queen's heavy footsteps coming up the stairway.

"I've got to go." The gnome put his hand over his head and—*whoosh*—disappeared in a puff of green smoke.

The queen came in and said, "Well, I'm sorry I gave you such a hard—Eileen! You did it! How did you do it?"

"Oh, that? I finished that job hours ago. I've been so bored in here, waiting around with nothing to keep me busy."

Is she telling the truth?

(No)

No.

"Maybe you really are the hardest-working girl in all of Ireland. You can come down to dinner now."

Was the queen satisfied?

(No)

No.

The queen said, "You did so well with that cloth, I've got another job for you. Come with me, dear."

She took Eileen up into the tower. There, in a corner, was the bolt of cloth from the day before and a pair of scissors, a needle, and some thread.

"You did so well with that cloth, I want you to make me a dress out of it. It had better fit me perfectly, dear."

"Oh, all right," Eileen said, "just let me take your measurements with this piece of thread—"

"Oh, no. If you're really the hardest-working girl in all of Ireland, you only need to look at me. You won't have any trouble making the dress to fit me perfectly. By the way, if it's not done by sundown tonight, it will be the worse for you!" She slammed the door.

Eileen sat down. She began to cry, "Oh, no, what am I going to do? My mother wanted to teach me about dresses. I never wanted to learn. What am I going to do?"

She heard a little voice. What did it say?

(I could help you.)

"I could help you."

"Oh, no, you couldn't help me. You helped me with the thread, you helped me with the cloth, but you couldn't help me with this."

"Oh, yes I could, but you'd have to promise to—"

"All right. I'll invite you to my wedding. Just help me."

Now the green gnome, and everyone else in the castle, knew that every morning after breakfast, the queen was accustomed to taking her royal bath. The gnome went into the corner of the tower room, put his hand up over his head and—*whoosh*—disappeared in a puff of green smoke. He reappeared in the queen's royal bathroom. The green gnome sneaked up to her bathtub, reached down into his pocket, and pulled out—

Does everybody here know what herbs are?

(Yes)

Yes. They're something like dried leaves.

He pulled out some of his magical gnome sleeping herbs and dropped them into the queen's bath water. Then he hid in the medicine chest.

The queen came in for her bath. She settled into the tub and fell fast asleep. The green gnome jumped out of the medicine chest and pulled out his measuring tape. He took some measurements of the queen, and then, just as the effect of the sleeping herbs was wearing off, he put his hand up over his head and—*whoosh*—disappeared in a puff of green smoke.

He reappeared back in the tower. He went over into the corner, and picked up the—what do you call those things?

(Scissors)

Scissors! He picked up the scissors. He picked up the—

(Needle)

Needle. He picked up the—

(Thread)

Thread!

The green gnome cut and sewed and made a beautiful dress. He was just tying off the last knot and hanging it up as the sun was dipping down into the sky. They heard the queen's heavy footsteps coming up the stairway.

"I've got to go," the green gnome said. "Don't forget your promise." He put his hand up over his head and—*whoosh*—disappeared into a puff of green smoke.

The queen came in. She said, "Well, I see you have made a dress, but the chances of its fitting me are quite remote. I'll try it on anyway."

The queen took off her everyday dress and tried on the dress the green gnome had made.

"Eileen! This is beautiful! I love it! It fits me perfectly! How did you do this?"

"Oh, it was no special trouble," Eileen said.

Is she telling the truth?

(No)

No.

"Maybe you really are the hardest-working girl in all of Ireland. You can come down to dinner now."

Was it an ordinary dinner that night?

(No)

No. It was a royal wedding.

Everybody was there. The king and queen were there. Eileen and her prince were there, of course. All the fine lords and ladies of the kingdom were there.

After the wedding ceremony, they had a great feast. Eileen and her prince sat at the head table. People were standing up and giving grand speeches and proposing toasts.

At the height of the proceedings, they all heard a knock out at the front gate of the castle.

The king said, "Guards, go see who that is. Probably some late arrival from another kingdom."

Then they all heard one of the guards shouting, "You! Get out of here! We don't allow people like you in here. Get out of here!"

The king said, "What's going on out there?"

"I'm sorry to trouble you with this, sire, but there's a little green—"

Just then the green gnome ran between the guard's legs and stopped in the center of the banquet hall, his hands on his hips, looking around at all the fine lords and ladies.

"Phewee!" All the fine guests were holding their noses and shouting, "Get him out of here. We don't allow people like him in here. Get him out of here!"

"No!" the green gnome shouted. "I've got a right to be here. None of you would be here tonight if I hadn't done what I did. Besides, Eileen invited me!"

"Oh!" Gasps and cries echoed through the banquet hall as eyes turned toward Eileen at the head table.

The queen said to Eileen, "This can't be true. Eileen, you didn't invite this disgusting person to your wedding, did you?"

Eileen looked at the green gnome. The green gnome looked at Eileen.

Eileen rose up to her full height and said in a voice loud enough for anyone to hear, "Yes, I did. I want you guards to seat him here beside me at the head table, in a place of honor."

When she said that, everyone said, "Oh, no, a gnome! We don't like a person like that. Get him out of here!"

One man yelled out, "Look how ugly he is. Look at his feet, for instance: they're so big and long."

"Well, I know that," the gnome said. "Do you think you're telling me something I don't know? I know they're not nice to look at, but they wouldn't look like this if they hadn't spent so much time working the pedal of a spinning wheel."

The prince stood up and turned to the queen. "Mother! I had no idea that's what happens to people's feet when they work on a spinning wheel! I would never want Eileen's feet to look like that!"

"Well, neither would I," said the queen. "Eileen, I know you love to work on the wheel, but I forbid you to ever touch a spinning wheel again as long as you live."

Eileen said, "Oh, all right."

Then someone shouted out, "Look at his fingers! That's another ugly thing about this gnome: his fingers are so long and thin."

"I know that," the gnome said. "I know they're not nice to look at, but they wouldn't look like this if they hadn't spent so much time working on the loom."

The prince said, "Mother! I had no idea! I would never want Eileen's fingers to look like that!"

"Neither would I," said the queen. "Eileen, I know you love the loom, but I must ask you never to touch one again as long as you live."

"It'll be a sacrifice," said Eileen, "but all right."

"The worst thing about a gnome," someone shouted out, "the worst thing is his nose. It's so long and red."

"Well, I know that," said the gnome, "but it wouldn't look like this if I hadn't stayed up so many nights, sewing dresses. I would fall asleep and the needle would prick my nose."

"Mother!" said the prince. "I would never want Eileen's nose to look like that!"

"Well, neither would I!" said the queen. "Eileen, I do love this dress, but I forbid you ever to sew another one."

"Oh, all right," said Eileen.

Everyone got what they wanted. The prince got to marry Eileen. Eileen got to marry the prince. The green gnome got to live in the castle. And the queen, she got a great many new dresses, all made by the little green gnome.

Congratulations! You are moving into some really interesting territory now. In this chapter, you began to grapple with the storyteller's task of uniting the inner and the outer worlds.

Have fun telling the two stories you learned in this chapter, and any others you add to your list. Now that you know some of the storyteller's skills, you may be hungry for material. In the next chapter we will dive into the subject of story sources, the raw materials for tales, and show you how to satisfy that hunger.

CHAPTER 3

Bringing the Story to Life

Selecting and Preparing Story Material

In this chapter we will:

- Learn how to locate, select, and prepare stories from inner and outer sources.
- Grapple with the issues of editing, revising, and recomposing material so that the stories we tell are consistent with the values we want to pass along to our children.

TYPES OF STORIES

We'll begin by looking at the types of stories you will want to tell. Then we will take a series of voyages that will show you how to convert material from these sources into tellable tales.

When we ask the question "What stories shall I tell my kids?," a bewildering array of possibilities faces us. Here are just a few.

personal experience	tales of wonder
tall tales	how and why stories
stories of here and now	funny stories
nursery stories	jokes
animal stories	poems
literary tales	recitations
folktales	songs
local legends	religious stories
ancient myths	teaching stories
creation stories	historical stories
fairy tales	dreams
hero tales	fables
supernatural stories	proverbs
ghost tales	fantasy

The same basic technique may be used to convert stories from any of these sources into tellable form. Let's divide these story types into broad categories and consider how to handle each group.

Like the storyteller's tools, story sources can be characterized as inner sources and outer sources. Here's a simplified list.

INNER SOURCES	OUTER SOURCES
personal memory	other storytellers
imagination	tapes and records
dreams	written sources

Let's examine each of these broad categories, concentrating on how we may locate, select, and prepare stories for telling.

INNER SOURCES

Personal Memory

LOCATING. The raw material for these stories is stored right in your own memory bank. You can go back into your personal memory and retrieve material for your stories as you did for the bike story in chapter 1.

The human memory has an incredible capacity. The problem is recalling information from it. The process of telling stories brings more and more memories into our awareness.

In Voyage 9 we make a general sweep through our childhood memories. We look at what we can turn up. Although this voyage is fairly lengthy, it will provide you with a wealth of detailed memory fragments that can later be expanded and combined to create stories. After this voyage, we will return to dealing with ways of selecting and preparing this material for telling. Incidentally, if you are taking this voyage with young children, remind them that although they have not lived as long as you have, they still have plenty of memories on which to build their stories.

VOYAGE 9

The Museum of Your Childhood

TIME: 15 minutes

GOAL: To use your five senses; to reexperience your childhood.

PREPARATION: Prepare the room. You may want to take this voyage lying down.

NOTE: Now is a good time to begin experimenting with the use of music in your voyages. A list of voyaging music appears in the Resources section. Pick something unobtrusive that will support your explorations rather than distract from them. For this voyage, pick something light and ethereal like Larkin's "O'Cean," flute music against a background of ocean sounds. Keep the sound level low. You want this music for background only. I carry a small portable tape recorder with earphones so I can have music with my voyages wherever I go. Earphones are ideal if you are voyaging alone; otherwise you can use an ordinary stereo system.

INSTRUCTIONS: The leader asks everyone to lie on the floor, blindfolded. The leader turns on some recorded music.

- The leader says, "Let's lie quietly for a moment, listening to the music, feeling safe and secure." (30-second pause)

- "The music is like a river, carrying us down into the inner world, back to the place where memories are stored."

- "See yourself standing before the door of a beautiful building. This is the Museum of Your Childhood, where all your childhood memories are carefully stored. A small group of appreciative listeners has come here with you. You can take them on a guided tour through your museum. If you would prefer to tour the museum on your own, that's OK too."

- "Open the door to your museum and enter the beautifully decorated hallway with five doors leading from it."

- "Notice that each of these doors is marked with a small sign. The first door is marked with a sign that says SIGHTS OF CHILDHOOD. The second door says SOUNDS OF CHILDHOOD, the third SMELLS OF CHILDHOOD, the fourth TASTES OF CHILDHOOD, and the fifth TOUCHES OF CHILDHOOD. This is a very elaborate museum. You have spared no expense to make exact replicas of things from your past."

- "Open the first door and walk into the room that displays the sights of your childhood: a life-size model of your childhood home, with your room exactly as it was, with every toy and every picture in its exact place. There is a walk-around model of your hometown, complete with the people who lived there. Using this room in the museum as a memory aid, spend some time reexploring the sights of your childhood."

- "If you are guiding your group of appreciative listeners through the museum, stop whenever you like and give them a full explanation of what they see and what it meant to you in your childhood. Convey your fascination with these familiar things from the past. If you see something you wish not to reexperience, simply let it go by and turn to something else. You may also give yourself this freedom in any of the other rooms in the museum. The tour is totally under your control."

- "If you are touring on your own, give yourself a running commentary, describing the things you see."
- "Take a few moments now and tour through all the sights of your childhood." (3-minute pause)
- "Know that you can come back to this room whenever you like and that you can stay for as long as you like when you do. For now, though, let's move along to the next room in your museum. Leave the room of sights behind and close the door behind you."
- "You are now in the hallway again. Walk to the next door, the door labeled SOUNDS OF CHILDHOOD. Open the door and enter. The black walls of the room are stacked with a very complex system of stereo speakers of all sizes and shapes. You have spared no expense in your museum to create a sound system that will surround you with exact reproductions of the sounds of your childhood. The lights in this room are dim, and there are several comfortable chairs around the room. Seat yourself in one. Invite your listeners to find seats."
- "There is a button on the right arm of your chair. When you push this button, a sound from your childhood will come through the speakers. You can listen to the sound as long as you like. When you push the button again, the sound will stop. After you listen to a sound, you can take a moment and describe it to your listeners or to yourself. When you push the button the next time, a new sound will come through the speakers. If any sound comes up that you don't wish to hear, feel free to push the button and move along to the next sound."
- "Take a few moments now to listen to the sounds from your past." (3-minute pause)
- "We must go on now. Finish listening to what is playing, then turn off the system by pushing the button a final time. You can come back to this room whenever you like. Stand up and leave the room of sounds. Close the door behind you."
- "Back in the hallway now, move to the third door, the

door marked SMELLS OF CHILDHOOD. Open the door and walk inside. Your listeners can come with you."

- "This room is similar in many ways to the room of sounds. Seat yourself in one of the comfortable chairs. There are fans of various sizes and shapes on the walls and the familiar button on the arm of your chair."

- "When you push this button, a smell from your childhood instantly fills the room. You have spared no expense to make a complete catalogue of the smells of your past and to ensure that each smell will be accurately reproduced. When you push the button a second time, the powerful fans will quietly whisk the smell from the room. Then you can give your listeners or yourself a description of what the smell meant to you in your childhood. When you push the button again, a new smell will fill the room. You can control the arrival and departure of these smells with your button. Take a few moments now to give yourself a tour through the smells of your childhood." (3-minute pause)

- "Finish with the smell you are now working on and whisk it from the room. You can come back to this room whenever you like and reexperience these smells for as long as you like. For now, though, it is time to move on. Leave the room of smells and close the door behind you."

- "Look across the hallway now to the door marked TASTES OF CHILDHOOD. Open the door and go inside."

- "This is a bright, colorful room. In the center is a table with comfortable chairs around it. Sit down. Invite your listeners to do the same."

- "On the table before you is an arrangement of serving dishes, each with a lid and a comfortable handle. A place has been set for you with a fresh napkin and eating utensils, as well as all the plates, bowls, glasses, and cups you will need."

- "You have spared no expense to duplicate exactly the tastes you experienced as a child. Each covered serving dish contains a different taste. Choose any serving dish you like, remove the lid, and serve yourself, placing the thing to be tasted on your plate or in your bowl or cup."

- "After you have tasted the item, replace the lid on the serving dish. As you do this, your plate, utensils, and taste buds will be instantly cleansed, and you will be ready to taste the next item. Invite your listeners to taste along with you."

- "Take as long as you like in between tastes to describe your feelings about what you just tasted from your past. When you are ready to go on to the next taste, select another serving dish and remove the lid, serving yourself as before. Tasting food in this room does not result in any weight gain in the outer world. Go ahead and reexperience the tastes of your childhood." (3-minute pause)

- "Finish with the taste you are working on now and replace the lid, cleaning the area so that everything will be in order when you next return. Stand up now and leave the room of tastes."

- "Enter the last door now, TOUCHES OF CHILDHOOD. In this room, you experience things from your past that you experienced with your sense of touch. This is a warmly lit, attractive room with no chairs. As you stand in the center of the room, you note that even though you are fully dressed, your skin is highly sensitized, able to detect the slightest sensation in the atmosphere of the room. The skin of your fingertips, hands, and face is very sensitive, but so is the skin in other parts of your body. Many people will want to be private about their experiences in this room. Leave your listeners outside in the hallway, if you wish."

- "There is a button on the floor by your right foot. When you push this button with your foot, your body will change to resemble exactly the body you had during an earlier period in your life. You will reexperience things you have stored in your museum having to do with the sense of touch. For instance, you may suddenly feel your body to be that of your eight-year-old self, and you may reexperience the thrill of riding your bike with your eight-year-old body."

- "You have spared no expense to make a complete catalogue of the things you have touched and been touched by in your life. These things can be as wispy as morning fog coming off the ocean, or as solid as the wood of a baseball bat or a concrete sidewalk against your bare knees."

- "When you push the button with your right foot a second time, the sensations will go away, and you will return to your present body. You can then talk about the memories the sensations call up for you as long as you like. When you push the button again, you will experience a new sensation. Let's take a few moments now to explore some touches. Begin by pushing the button with your foot to experience the first one."

- "Move through these sensations at whatever rate seems appropriate to you. If you encounter a touch you wish not to reexperience, simply push the button and move along to the next one. You may want to return to these disturbing touches later and confront what they mean to you. For now, though, just take a brief tour of some different bodily sensations." (3-minute pause)

- "Complete the touch you are now working on and push the floor button to return to your own body. Leave the room of touches and close the door behind you."

- "Back in the hallway, look again at these doors of perception within which you've stored so many memories. Realize what a great treasure it is to have a museum like this to enjoy and to learn about your past from. Leave your museum now, knowing that you can return whenever you like. If listeners are with you, bid them a respectful goodbye, and allow the music to bring you back out of memory, back into your body lying on the floor with your eyes closed. Take a moment now to review the banquet of sights, sounds, smells, tastes, and touches you reexperienced in your museum."

- "When you are ready to come back into the room, rub your hands together, then rub your face, remove your blindfold, and, when you are ready, open your eyes and come back into the room."

- "Take a few moments to share some of the most vivid memories of the voyage with each other."

- "The voyage is now complete."

FEEDBACK: A father said, "I was very moved by going back into my childhood bedroom and playing with my old toys. I was clearly able to see and feel things that I hadn't thought about in years."

"I sat up in the treehouse we had in Indiana and ate crab apples," said a boy.

A woman reported, "The smell of my grandmother's perfume was worth the journey all by itself."

A man admitted, "I felt a little guilty that such a grandiose museum should be built just for my life. When I thought about having spared no expense to equip each of the rooms, I wondered if this wasn't a terrible waste of resources that could be better used for something else. Then I realized that it is really true: we each do have a museum inside where memory has spared no expense to capture and hold everything that has happened. We are foolish if we don't use this resource."

FOLLOW-UP TO VOYAGE 9: The tour of your museum is not designed to serve up stories for you on a silver platter. It is meant to stimulate your memory and allow you to reexperience things from the past. It is a good way to locate personal memories. Jean Houston gives an excellent explanation of this in her book *The Possible Human*.

Once you open the door to your museum, you can wander around in there and find the beginning places for thousands of stories.

SELECTING. The act of selecting a story to tell is not a random decision. There is probably something in that story that we wish, consciously or unconsciously, to communicate. Be aware, then, of the subjects that you choose. In my work with divorced and separated fathers, I found that these men wanted to tell their children stories of their own youth, but avoided telling stories of their present family life.

It is important to tell different kinds of stories to our children, not just stories that brag about our own exploits and adventures. There is tremendous value in children hearing about the achievements of their parents, but I feel strongly that we should also tell them about our wounds and our defeats, about times when we were afraid and unsure of our place in the world, as they sometimes are.

Kids can smell a rat. If your story is meant to manipulate them in some way—to shame them into getting good grades like you did, for example—the story-listening will end very quickly. If you give a well-rounded accounting of your life, your children will admire your strengths, accept your weaknesses, and draw their own conclusions.

PREPARING. In Voyage 2 in chapter 1, we learned the process of preparing a personal-experience story for telling. To review:

- Go back into memory and retrieve the memory you want to prepare for telling (as we did in our bike ride and fire stories). "Film" the memory, using the daydreaming technique.
- Run the film in your mind.
- Use your outer tools to describe to the listeners what you are reexperiencing using all of your senses.

Here's a story my kids love to hear. Read the story aloud, noting how I used memories of various body sensations to allow the listener to enter the physical reality of the tale.

How Daddy Saved Himself from Falling Off a Cliff

When my friend Steve Draper and I were hiking out in northern California, I had a frightening experience.

We were walking along a loose shelf of rock up on a mountainside, rock called "talus." It slides underneath your feet every time you take a step. I was not very well prepared. I was wearing sandals that day, and it was really hard to get a grip on the rock. I was moving pretty slow, and Steve got ahead of me, maybe a hundred yards or so.

Walking on my own, I came to a place where there was a steep drop-off, maybe two hundred feet, to the Trinity River in the valley below. I started to make my way across that loose rock when I lost my footing and the rock started to slide away underneath me. I put my hands out to steady myself, but there was nothing to grab on to. It was then that I realized I had created a tiny avalanche. That whole section of rocky mountainside had started to slide under me.

The sliding rock started to pick up more and more speed and was carrying me downhill, right to the very edge of that cliff. I started to get pretty scared because I realized that if I got swept out over the edge of the cliff, I was going to fall two hundred feet into the river below. And that river was only about three feet deep and filled with rocks. I knew I would never survive a fall like that.

Then I looked up ahead and saw a small juniper tree, about five feet high, growing at the edge of the cliff. I figured if I could just work my way over to that tree, I could grab ahold of it and save myself.

So I scrambled across the moving rock with my hands and feet, and as the rock carried me up to the edge of the cliff, I was just able to reach out and grab ahold of that tree.

To this day, I don't know if it was my hands or my head that broke the hornets' nest in that tree. But there I was, hanging on to that tree on the edge of the cliff, with those white-faced hornets swarming all over me, stinging me like all get-out!

They were all over me: they were in my hair, in my beard, inside my clothes, and just stinging me like crazy.

Somehow I managed to turn around and scramble my way back up the mountainside. The little avalanche I had made had almost stopped, but with every step I took, it would start up again, and I felt the rock sliding under me as I scrambled up the loose rock.

Of course, I didn't get away from those hornets. They were still stinging me! They were just along for the ride, stinging me no matter where I went. At last I got back up to the trail on the rock shelf where I had started. I had lost one of my sandals on the way down, but I still had one, so I took it off and used it as a hornet-swatter, trying to kill those darn things. I took off my shirt, and the inside was just covered with hornets. I started pulling them out of my hair and beard, and they were stinging my fingers as I pulled them off. Fortunately, there was a pretty stiff wind up there on the shelf, and it blew most of the hornets away.

I slumped down on the ground and yelled for Steve. A few moments later he came back along the trail. At first he couldn't figure out why I was lying on the ground. When he got closer, he saw that my whole body was covered with red welts, swelling to the size of grapes. I must have had fifty or sixty hornet stings on me. I was hot and weak, and my head was throbbing—not just my head, but my whole body was throbbing with pain.

When I caught my breath, I told Steve what had happened.

"We've got to get you down to the river fast," he said.

He helped me up and we backtracked down the trail to a place where a stream had worn a gully in the mountainside. There wasn't any water in it then. We saw it was the fastest way down. We half climbed, half slid down that gully until we got to the river.

I was pretty woozy by then, but Steve took me and threw me into the river and waded in beside me, holding me up. I ducked my head under the cool water and just floated there for about a half hour. It felt so good to be in that cool running water, and I guess it carried the hornet poison out of me.

After a while, I crawled up on a little shady ledge there by the river and lay there, exhausted. I felt pretty weak for the rest of the day, but my headache was gone, and my body temperature had come down, and after a good night's sleep I was as good as new.

If it hadn't been for that juniper tree and if Steve hadn't been there to get me down to the river like he did, I don't know what would have happened to me.

Imagination

Stories from the imagination, made up on the spur of the moment, are the second largest category of stories we tell around our house.

Although we will be working with the same basic technique we have been using all along, the normal steps of locating, selecting, and preparing become muddled here. In terms of locating and selecting, you might say that it's the story that chooses you, not the other way around. As for preparing, there is no preparation; you are simply "winging it." However, there are several tricks of the trade that can help you make the best of what the muse offers you.

Here's how I begin. When one of my kids asks me for a story, I immediately go into my imagination and locate the very first image that comes my way. Maybe it is an old man in a blue bathrobe. Why did I get that image? Who cares? The point is, this is my starting place.

"Long ago, there lived a man in a blue bathrobe." There's my first line. From there on out, I strive to be open to whatever connections come up. Of course, I don't have to use all the material that offers itself; I can select as I go along.

When creating stories from scratch, I am not just pulling things out of the air and saying anything that comes into my head. That might be an interesting experiment in spontaneous, stream-of-consciousness performing, but it would not be storytelling. If our dreams are to take shape as stories, they must fall within certain parameters. Fortunately, those parameters are broad enough to make plenty of room for improvisation. If you have a good grasp of the elements of story structure, you can create a completely original and satisfying story on the spot.

Let's take a look at the basic elements of story structure. A story has four parts: the invitation, the beginning, the middle, and the end.

The *invitation* can be as simple as asking, "Would you like to hear a story?," or it can be a more formal ritual, like lighting a candle. The storytelling equation from chapter 1 reminds us that the teller can't just go barging into the listener's inner world. If the teller speaks without the listener's consent, the story will never reach the inner world. Do not neglect the invitation.

The *beginning* is a crucial point of transition from the outer world to the inner world. The teller and the listener must make the leap together. People have developed many different formulas and methods for beginning a story. Phrases as simple as "once upon a time" and "a long, long time ago" are common story beginnings. These words flip a switch in the brains of our listeners. They prepare themselves to shift their way of perceiving the world. Not the words, but the manner of the storyteller is vital here.

The *middle* is the meat of the story. The storyteller reveals the problem and begins to work toward its resolution. Through all the twists and turns of the plot, the middle of the story is headed in one direction: toward the end.

The *end,* like the beginning, is a vital transition point. It returns listeners to the outer world. A listener abandoned in midstory, in a story that has no conclusion, will feel cheated and unsatisfied.

The last line of the story, like the first, may be somewhat formal. "They lived happily ever after" and "That was the last anyone ever saw of that old witch" are examples of standard story endings. Garrison Keillor began his monologues on the *Prairie Home Companion* with the familiar line "Well, it's been a quiet week in Lake Woebegon" and ended always with "And that's the news from Lake Woebegon." These phrases functioned like signals for the listeners. Listeners always knew when the story was beginning and when it was ending.

Content is as important as structure in stories from the imagination. Stories are about problems. If there were no problems, there would be no stories.

For example: "Long ago there lived a king and queen in a castle. All went well in that kingdom, everyone always treated everyone else with the greatest respect and courtesy, and there was never any reason for anyone to feel troubled about anything. The end." That's not a story, that's a weather report. A story has adversity, struggle, and longing in it.

As in: "Long ago, there lived a king and queen in a castle. There was one problem: the queen couldn't have a child. She felt very bad about this because, as everyone knew, one of the duties of a queen is to give children to the kingdom. So she called the old witchy woman to her and said, 'Can you help me?'

" 'Ah, yes,' the old woman said. 'Here are my instructions. You must listen carefully and do exactly as I say.' "

And you're off and running.

When I am putting stories together for my kids, I like to start with a setup like this: "Once there lived a boy who would eat nothing but vanilla ice cream."

Then I introduce the big problem: "Then one day his parents found out he was allergic to dairy products.

" 'I'm sorry,' his mother said, 'you won't be allowed to eat any more ice cream.'

"Well, what could the boy do?"

Now I have set up the boy's problem and challenged him to find a solution. For the problem, I like to use something my kids can relate to.

A story is a time-factored work of art. It starts at a beginning and moves through to an end. It progresses always forward, to a resolution of some sort. There may be many digressions in the middle of the story, but every line should move the story ahead and keep the listener asking, "What happened next?"

Story motifs are useful tools. A motif is a single element of a story, like the losing of the glass slipper in "Cinderella." Stith Thompson's classic reference work *The Folktale* lists hundreds of common stories by type and motif. Thompson compares motifs from cultures around the world.

Here's an example of how story motifs fit together. I made up this story one night for my daughter. It involves a character we've used in many other stories, the Tooth-Fairy-in-Training.

Ear Wax

One day the Tooth-Fairy-in-Training was having trouble with ear wax. So she complained to her supervisor, the Senior Tooth Fairy, Minerva.

Minerva looked at her and said, "Look here, kid. You shouldn't be digging around in your ears with your fingers and stuff. You can use one of these Q-Tips to clean up the wax on the outside of your ears, but don't be sticking stuff down into your ear. Got it?"

"OK," the Tooth-Fairy-in-Training said. And she followed Minerva's advice. The problem was, she collected so much ear wax, she didn't know what to do with it. She collected about a cup a week and couldn't bring herself to throw it away. It just sat there in a Tupperware container in her refrigerator.

Then, one day, she had an inspiration. She took out her wax—she had about a gallon of it by then—and she used her clay-making tools and made herself a beautiful set of waxed golden wings, about two feet long.

She strapped the wings onto her back and up she flew,

higher and higher. This was wonderful! She had recycled her ear wax; she was flying around having a great time, making her tooth-fairy deliveries—when she made a mistake.

She flew too close to the sun, and the sun melted her wings. The Tooth-Fairy-in-Training started falling down, down, hundreds of feet. The ground was coming up fast.

At this point in my telling of the story, my daughter interrupted. "I know what happens. Some birds catch the Tooth Fairy on their wings and carry her safely to the ground," she said.

That was fine with me. I hadn't really known how I was going to get the Tooth-Fairy-in-Training out of that fix anyway. I realized what a good use my daughter had made of story motifs. Just a few weeks before, I had told my kids an Iroquois creation story about the woman who fell down from the sky-world and the birds who caught her on their backs. My daughter recognized that motif, and she spontaneously fit it into a new story. The other motif working in "Ear Wax" is from the Greek myth about Icarus.

CHARACTERIZATION. Developing characters is another fun part of these homemade stories. In our family, we often create a character, like the Tooth-Fairy-in-Training, that we can include in our stories night after night. Anything that happens to that character will interest us.

One character we use a lot is Sweetnosia. Here's how her story started.

Sweetnosia

Long ago, there lived a princess named Doorknobia. She was a very nice-looking girl except for one thing: she had a big round nose that looked like a doorknob. So everyone called her Doorknobia, not noticing how it hurt her feelings.

One night one of the servants in the castle got confused as he was opening a door. He grabbed ahold of Doorknobia's nose instead and gave it a good, hard twist.

"Owwwwww!" she screamed.

"Oh, my princess, I'm so sorry," the servant said.

"That's it!" Doorknobia hollered. "I've had it!"

She went down to the river and got her canoe and paddled all the way up Wizard Creek until she came to the place where the wizards lived. There was a wizard there for every part of the body. They were specialists, you see.

The wizard who worked on ears lived inside an ear-shaped hill. The wizard who worked on chins lived inside a chin-shaped hill. The wizard who worked on elbows lived inside an elbow-shaped hill. At last Doorknobia found herself standing in front of a hill shaped like a huge nose. Where the nostrils should be, there were two doors, one marked IN, the other marked OUT.

She was just about to knock on the IN door when she heard a huge sneeze from inside the hill, and the door blew open. There sat the wizard of noses. He wore a blue wizard's hat and a blue wizard's bathrobe, all covered with tiny designs of noses. He had a pretty good honker on himself, too, I'll tell ya, and he was wiping it with a big blue handkerchief.

"What can I do for you, my princess?" he asked, recognizing her immediately.

"I want a new nose," Doorknobia said.

The wizard understood. He put on his glasses and motioned her toward him. "Well, all right," he said. "Come on over here in the light so I can get a good look at you."

The wizard took Doorknobia's face in his hands and turned it gently from side to side, looking at her nose from all angles.

"Yep," he said at last, "you've got quite a beak there, don'tcha? Let's take a look at what I've got back in the stockroom."

He disappeared through a narrow doorway and came back in a moment, carrying a silver tray full of noses.

"Take a look at these," he offered. "Go ahead, pick your nose—I mean, pick out something ya like."

Doorknobia was so excited it took her about ten minutes to decide. She finally picked out a very sweet, finely proportioned nose, just turned up slightly at the end.

"Shall I put it in a bag for ya, or do ya want to wear it home?" the wizard asked, but when he saw Doorknobia's shocked expression he quickly added, "Just joking."

The wizard assembled his tools: a large blue handkerchief and a can of sneezing powder.

"Now, this won't hurt a bit," he muttered, placing the nose Doorknobia had chosen into the handkerchief. "Now, you just hold still, and let me sprinkle some of this sneezing powder onto your present nose. When you feel like you're ready to sneeze, just press this handkerchief with your new nose in it up to your face, and sneeze through your new nose. You got that? There's nothing to it; I've done this operation thousands of times."

Doorknobia stood still, holding the handkerchief with her new nose as the wizard sprinkled the powder on her old nose, and then she did just as he had said: she sneezed through her new nose. She ran and looked into the mirror: There, in the center of her face, was the sweetest, cutest little turned-up nose you would ever want to see.

"Oh," Doorknobia said, "I love it! Is it permanent?"

"Of course," the wizard answered. "It's there for the rest of your life. Unless, of course, you change your mind, in which case you'll get a money-back guarantee."

"How can I ever thank you enough?" Doorknobia asked.

"You can't, my dear. Just go back to the castle and enjoy your new nose."

Doorknobia reached down to open the door and felt something familiar—it was her old nose! The wizard had used her old nose for a doorknob.

"Just recycling," the wizard said.

Well, Doorknobia got back in her canoe and paddled back to the castle.

When Doorknobia's mother saw her she said, "Welcome back, my dear, sweet Doorkno— Wait a minute! You've changed your nose. I never realized how unsightly that old nose was. We won't call you Doorknobia ever again. From now on, we will call you Sweetnosia."

And that's exactly what they did.

STORY GAMES. Games can also provide structures to help create stories. Here are two games we play at our house, "Royal Inventor" and "Wizard." Have fun making up some more of your own.

"Royal Inventor" began when I once told my kids a story about a king who wanted something to eat that was hot and cold at the same time. The problem was solved when one of his subjects brought him a hot fudge sundae. This story evolved into a game in which the king makes more and more outrageous demands, challenging the royal inventor to create something entirely new each and every day.

Here's an example of how the story game works.

Salty and Sweet at the Same Time

One day the king called in his royal inventor and said, "I want something to taste that will be both salty and sweet at the same time. And by the way, if it's not done by sundown tonight, you're out of a job."

The inventor went home to his family. They lived in a small

cottage near the castle that the king had provided for them. It was just after breakfast, and the inventor's wife and his young son and daughter were just clearing away the breakfast things.

"Mary, you may as well start packing our things up. We've got to be out of the kingdom by sundown," he told his wife.

"What does the king want this time?" she asked.

"Oh, he wants something that tastes both sweet and salty at the same time. I don't know why he insists on giving me these impossible assignments."

"Don't worry," Mary said. "You'll think of something. You always do. Why don't you just go out into your work-shop and putter around out there? Maybe something will come to you."

Well, something did come to him: his two children.

The inventor's wife took her children aside and said, "Kids, your father is very worried, and he needs your help. Go out there and see if you can give him some ideas."

The boy and the girl ran out to the workshop. There was their father, sitting on his stool by the workbench where he made all his inventions.

"What am I going to do, kids? The king keeps coming up with these stupid ideas for inventions. Today he wants me to make something both salty and sweet at the same time."

"You can do it, Dad," the girl said. "You've had harder assignments than this before. Remember when the king wanted you to make a shoe that could work as both a boat and a kite at the same time?"

"That's right," her brother said. "Or how about the time he wanted you to make a hat out of birds that would cool him in the summer and warm him in the winter?"

"You're right, kids," the inventor said, getting down to work. "Now, what could we make that is both salty and sweet at the same time?"

[At this point in the story I ask my kids: "Well, what could they do, guys?" The kids brainstorm and offer suggestions.

"How about mixing up honey and salt?"

"What about ocean water, that's salty!"

"Or how about combining ocean water and bees! Maybe you could take some bees out on a boat out in the ocean and have them get all salty."

"I know—tears! People's tears are salty."

"Yes! You could get the king to cry and then have him taste something sweet—"

This goes on for five minutes or so, just letting the kids brainstorm. Then I pick one of their suggestions to make a solution. The best solutions in this game force relationships between seemingly unrelated ideas.]

The inventor listened to his kids' suggestions and then he got an idea!

That evening, just as the sun was dipping down, the inventor went up to the king's throne room. The king sat there, waiting for the new invention.

"Come forward, royal inventor," the king said. "You have never failed me. Have you found a way for me to taste something sweet and salty at the same time?"

"Yes, sire. But you must ask the queen to come in so she can help."

"Of course. Guards, call the queen."

The queen entered and asked the royal inventor, "Is it one of your inventions again? I just love your inventions."

"Yes, your majesty," the inventor said, "but I will need your help." He drew the queen aside and said, "Your highness, when I give you a signal, I want you to kiss your husband on the lips."

"I would be delighted," the queen said.

Then the inventor began to tell the king a sad story about a boy lost at sea who was marooned on a desert island with only his dog and a copy of *Robinson Crusoe* to keep him company.

The king grew misty-eyed. "*Robinson Crusoe*," he muttered. "I loved that book when I was a boy."

The inventor went on to tell how the boy and his dog learned to survive on the island. Every night, the boy would read his dog the story of Robinson Crusoe by the fire. The king was touched. His eyes were damp with tears.

The inventor told how the dog died one night of old age, just as the boy was reading the last chapter of *Robinson Crusoe*. The king began crying. Large, fat tears rolled down his face. Then the inventor told how the boy buried his dog on the beach and read the last chapter of *Robinson Crusoe* over the poor dog's grave. The king was crying hard now, his shoulders shaking and tears streaming down his face. Then the inventor told how the boy laid the book down on the sand and planted a wooden cross over the dog's grave. A wave came rushing up and swept the book out to sea.

When the king heard that, he wailed and sobbed.

"I loved that book," he said, big tears running down his cheeks and into his mouth.

Then the inventor gave the queen a signal.

She stood before the king, wrapped him in her arms, and gave him a sweet kiss on the lips. "It's all right, dear. We still have your copy of *Robinson Crusoe* in the Royal Library."

The king looked up. "We do? Why, that's wonderful! I'm going to read it tonight—but wait!" The king smacked his lips. "Inventor! You did it! I tasted the sweetness of the queen's kiss and the saltiness of my own tears at the same time! You did it! You're a genius! How do you think of this all by yourself?"

"It's all in a day's work, sire," the inventor said modestly.

"Go home and get a good night's sleep," the king said. "Tonight I am going to sit up and read *Robinson Crusoe* while I think of a new invention for you to make tomorrow."

"Gee, thanks," the inventor said. And then he went home to his family. His children met him at the door of the cottage.

"Did it work, Dad?" they asked him.

"Well, of course, kids. But I never could have done it without your help."

The kids ran off to play, and the inventor went in to help his wife get dinner on the table.

"How did things go today?" she asked.

"Oh, fine," the inventor said, "but I'm kind of worried about tomorrow. That crazy king! There's no telling what kind of ridiculous thing he's going to want me to invent tomorrow."

"Oh, don't worry, dear," his wife said. "You'll think of something. You always do."

The structure of this game assures us that the inventor is going to come up with a solution to the problem. When we begin the game, though, we have no idea what the solution's going to be. We have fun brainstorming and letting intuition guide us to an invention that is a distillation of the kids' suggestions.

It is always the inventor's kids who come up with the ideas and the inventor who puts them together. We have been playing this game for a few years now, and I find that as my kids get older, the king's requests become more outrageous, and the inventor's solutions even more inventive.

"Wizard," another story game that we play, was invented by

my friend Bill Mettler, who has kindly allowed me to borrow it. "Wizard" is also about problem solving. The tables are turned here. The parent plays the kid, and the kid takes the role of the all-knowing Wizard.

Wizard	*Kid:*	(*mimes picking up a telephone and dialing*) Brngggggg. Brngggggg.
	Wizard:	(*mimes picking up the phone*) Hello?
	Kid:	Is this the Wizard?
	Wizard:	Yeah. What's the problem?
	Kid:	It's my parents. When I come home from school they want me to do my homework before I go out and play, but by the time I finish my homework it's dinnertime, and by the time dinner's over it's dark, and then I have to get ready for bed, and there's no time to play out in the yard except on weekends. I don't think that's fair.
	Wizard:	Well, well, maybe you could make a deal. Why don't you tell your parents that you promise to do your homework after dinner if you can play outside before dinner?
	Kid:	Great idea, Wizard! Thanks! I'll try it. (*Mimes hanging up the phone*) (*This is the end of the first conversation.*)
	Kid:	(*mimes dialing*) Hello, Wizard?
	Wizard:	How's it going?
	Kid:	Your idea didn't work too well.
	Wizard:	What do you mean?
	Kid:	Well, I made a deal with my parents, and they let me play outside before dinner, but when I did my homework after dinner, it took so long that I didn't get to bed on time. My parents got real grumpy. They said your idea didn't work and I'll have to go back to doing my homework as soon as I come home from school. Can you give me another idea?
	Wizard:	All right. Look, how long does it take for you to do your homework?
	Kid:	About half an hour. Or sometimes maybe an hour because it takes me so long to settle down and do it because I am feeling so mad about not being able to play outside.

Wizard: Look, if you get right down to work, you could do your homework in half an hour. You'd have the rest of the time to play and everyone would be a lot happier. Wait a minute! I've got another idea. How long do you spend on the school bus in the afternoon?

Kid: About twenty minutes.

Wizard: Great! Why don't you get started on your homework while you're riding on the bus? When you come home, you can launch right into the rest of it and get it done quickly!

Kid: OK, Wizard, I'll give it a try. (*Mimes hanging up the phone*)
(*This ends the second conversation.*)

Kid: Hey, Wiz!

Wizard: Yeah? How did it go with your homework?

Kid: Great! I started working on it on the school bus and almost finished it. When I got home it only took me fifteen minutes to get to the end! I had all the rest of the time to go outside and play. I didn't realize how much time I was wasting by grumping and complaining when I could have been outside playing. Thanks a lot, Wizard!

Wizard: No problem. Call me anytime. (*Mimes hanging up*)

"Wizard" is a great two-part story game. It lets parents see problems from the kid's point of view. The game is very empowering for the child. The child is responsible for finding a solution. Notice that the structure of the story makes the first attempt at a solution a failure or a marginal success at best. The structure presses the Wizard to find an even better solution.

Dreams

There is an intimate connection between stories and dreams. When your kids are listening to one of your stories, they are in the same state as when they are dreaming at night. Remember what I said before, using the iceberg metaphor: storytelling reaches beyond the surface of normal waking consciousness, delving into the area we visit when we dream at night. So storytelling presents itself as an ancient technique for experiencing the dreaming state while we are awake.

My dreams do not provide me with perfectly crafted stories,

served up on a silver platter and ready to tell. I have learned some techniques, though, that have helped me use my dream world as a valuable source for stories. Some of these techniques came from a quirky, insightful book called *The Jungian-Senoi Dreamwork Manual* by Strephon Kaplan Williams. Williams's book is listed in the Resources section, as are two other books that may help: *A Little Course in Dreams* by Robert Bosnak, and *Working with Dreams* by Montague Ullman and Nan Zimmerman.

LOCATING. Everyone dreams. The average person has five dream periods a night. Most of us don't remember all our dreams, and some of us rarely remember any of them. You can improve your ability to remember your dreams by using these three techniques:

1. Prepare your memory. Before you fall asleep, give your internal computer these instructions: "I will dream. I will remember my dreams. Once a dream is completed, I will wake up, write down the dream, and then fall back to sleep." Image yourself typing these instructions on a computer keyboard and seeing them displayed on the computer screen. You will be surprised at how effective this technique can be.

2. Prime the pump. The dream world is highly susceptible to suggestion. Reading mythology or fairy tales just before you go to sleep can supply your dream world with rich and dramatic images.

3. Record your dreams. Don't trust yourself to remember them. Unless you write them down, all but the most vivid dreams may be gone by morning. Keep a spiral-bound notebook, a pen, and a bedside light within reach of your bed. Whether you wake up in the middle of the night or in the morning, follow this procedure: Begin writing as fast as possible. Do not attempt to organize or edit anything; record everything that comes to mind, even if it makes no sense. It may be just a string of words and phrases: "Cliff, bookcase, Indiana Jones. It falls in the green water." These brief notes will help you reconstruct the dream when you are fully awake in the morning. If you still have trouble recalling a dream, simply lie quietly and try to hold in your mind even the smallest fragment of the dream. Then other parts of it will come flowing back. This technique requires finesse. It's like trying to shovel smoke with a pitchfork in the wind.

SELECTING. Once you have rendered a dream in written form, you can recompose it as a story, or use an image in it as a departure point for an original story. When I was writing my Bread Sister Trilogy, a series of three historical novels about women on the Pennsylvania frontier, I often found that images from dreams would find their way into my work.

Here is a dream my daughter recalled.

A Dream of Wings

I was running in my backyard with my stuffed animal "Half and Half" in my arms, and her wings started to flap! Then she rose out of my arms, and she started to grow bigger and bigger and bigger, so I could ride on her back. We flew away in the cotton clouds, and we came back in time for dinner.

That's not a bad story in itself. It also provides a departure point for other stories about flights with "Half and Half."

When we bring our dreams into the outer world, they become like living things. When we tell a story, we are calling it to life.

Not all the dreams we encounter are pleasant ones. Both of my children have been troubled by nightmares off and on throughout their childhood. Every parent has probably sat up at 3:00 A.M., bleary-eyed, reassuring a child for the fifteenth time that the shadow in the corner is not a monster. It's certainly upsetting to see a kid terrified like this.

If you tell your kids scary stories, they may have scary dreams. Whether their nightmares originate from stories you tell them or from their own inner world, it is our responsibility as parents to give our children the tools to cope with these nighttime terrors. Here are a few techniques that can help.

Prevention is the best cure. Be selective about the stories you tell just before bedtime. I know, I know. The Jungian psychologists say it's important to confront your shadow and deal with your inner witches. But sometimes I just get tired of sitting up all night with this sort of thing. Watching TV can be troubling to small children. Even if the TV show is a harmless movie, the commercials, the news, and the powerful images of the television world can play havoc with your kids' dreams. Our family has learned to be very selective about the kinds of things we watch, especially before bedtime.

If your children are having bad dreams regularly, you can give them an escape hatch by using the old folk remedy: "If you put your shoes underneath the bed with the toes facing opposite directions, you won't have any bad dreams." This gives them the power to control the images.

You can use the same ploy with an imaginary magic wand or magic ring that the child holds as he or she falls asleep. Psychologist Doris Brett has a good discussion of this in her book *Annie Stories*.

Confront the nightmare. The Senoi taught their children to reenter their dreams and bring them to resolution. A common recurring dream is being chased by a monster. If the monster is chasing you again and again, something is stuck somewhere. The way to move the story along is to speak to the monster, ask it why it is chasing you. Offer to make a deal. Threaten to kick it out of your dream world. The monster may become a potential ally. Here is an example of a recurring nightmare of my own that I cured through dream reentry. This is from my dream notebook of February 1987.

> *The Tunnel*
>
> Very frightening nightmare—I am in a narrow underground tunnel, crawling down to get a bunch of diamonds. No way do I want to go down there. I am afraid of the claustrophobia, of getting stuck down there. I get stuck. I can't move backward or forward. I start yelling.

At this point, I woke up. I was prepared to resolve the situation by dream reentry. I was still feeling the frightening effects of the dream, so I got up and walked around the bed a few times; then, determined to ride it out, I got back into bed. I held in my mind the image and the feeling of being stuck in the tunnel and screaming. I fell asleep instantly. Here's what my dream notebook records:

> I am in the tunnel, screaming. I force myself ahead. I somehow know that there is a room at the end of the tunnel big enough for me to turn around in so I can come out head first. But I'm scared to go ahead anymore. Then I hear Jesse, my son, yelling for me. I realize that he is in the room at the end of the tunnel and I have to crawl down and get him. I crawl ahead and find him in the small, underground room. There is just enough space to turn around. I crawl out head first, pushing him ahead of me. When I get up to the surface, I realize that if Jesse hadn't yelled, I would still be stuck down there.

My recurring nightmare ended because I had brought the situation to resolution through dream reentry.

Another technique is to rewrite the dream, by falling asleep with the intention of redirecting the nightmare so that it sets the dream off in a more positive direction. For instance, we can speak to a monster and have it answer us so that the dream allows us to have an opportunity to address the thing that is chasing us.

These are only a few of the fascinating techniques that have been developed to help parents and kids get through the nightmare situation.

PREPARING. Now that we have recorded and selected the dreams we want to work with, how do we prepare them for telling?

Whenever we tell about a dream, we alter it. We all begin editing our dreams as soon as we tell them. Monte Ullman says:

> Dreams do not lie, but liars dream. What we call a dream is actually a pale facsimile of the original episode of dreaming. When we pull a fish out of the sea, we can't expect to see it, feel it, and understand its way of life as if it were still swimming about freely, but we can learn something about it before it dies.
>
> The remembered dream is like that flapping fish we were lucky enough to have caught. We have to do something with it or throw it back into the sea. That brings up the first and perhaps most important difference between the way we relate to a dream while asleep and while awake. In our sleep we have no choice but to attend to the pictures which appear before us and involve us in the action. We have the option of attending or not attending to the *memory* of these nocturnal images. Should we choose to attend to the dream, we become the accidental beneficiaries of a vast amount of research done during the night shift while our body was deciding how safe it was to remain asleep. As I see it, we do not dream a dream for the benefit of the waking state, but the waking state can nevertheless benefit from it. If, then, we are fortunate enough to recall the dream on awakening, we have the opportunity to look at the amount of information about ourselves that has been amassed and to dive back into the unfamiliar waters where the dream came from and learn more about the habitat that shaped the images.

Ullman developed an effective technique for experiencing dreams, not so much for the purpose of dream analysis, but instead for what he calls "dream appreciation." Dream appreciation means returning ourselves to the experience of the dream and using this as our source for selecting what parts of the dream are most useful to us. In many ways, this is similar to the movie-camera technique we have used throughout this book. For a full discussion of dream appreciation in a small-group setting, see Ullman's book. We can become the "accidental beneficiaries" of our dreams if we allow dream images to work in our stories.

The mechanics of telling a dream are not much different from telling a personal experience story. You simply recall it and tell what you see. If you are working from a dream notebook, you produce an edited version of the dream. You can use this version as the basis for your film clip.

OUTER SOURCES

Other Tellers

The most important outer source for stories is other storytellers. Listen to the people around you, at home, in your neighborhood, at work, and at school. You are surrounded by lots of unconscious storytelling every day. Even in our highly literate society, people still depend upon word of mouth for the bulk of the information they receive each day. Stories are best learned by ear. Seek out the tellers.

LOCATING. Listen to the conversations of the people around you with a special ear for their style of telling. The best way to get stories from your relatives, for example, is to prime the pump by telling a few you know. Alternately, get out the photo album and ask questions. A helpful guide to getting family stories is *Your Life and Times: An Oral History Handbook* by Stephen and Julia Arthur. This workbook shows you how to put family stories on tape. Headings about work, school, and other subjects help guide your interviews.

Seek out the storytellers in your community, too. You can locate old-timers by contacting the local historical society. Most towns have a few local historians who will fill your ear with fascinating lore about local things.

The library is another important local resource. Libraries in America have kept storytelling as a performing art alive for over one hundred years. Many libraries host a weekly story hour for children. Many a librarian is a good teller with an ear for what kids like. The local library may also know of local professional or semiprofessional tellers.

The information in the Resources section can also help you find other tellers in your area. An ever-widening network of local storytelling guilds provides tellers with places to meet. Some informal guilds meet for story-swapping sessions in members' homes. Other guilds are quite sophisticated, with newsletters, annual festivals, and year-round calendars of story-related events. If there is no storytelling group in your area, why not start one? Bring other tellers out of the woodwork.

The storytelling renaissance has fostered many fine professional storytellers who have elevated tale spinning to a fine art. The NAPPS newsletter is another great resource.

Consider taking your family to a storytelling festival. It is a remarkable experience to hear a teller hold an audience of twenty thousand spellbound. The National Storytelling Festival, held in Jonesborough, Tennessee, is the great-granddaddy of them all.

SELECTING. Selecting tales from those told by another teller brings up some special considerations and ethical issues. There is a huge controversy now in the storytelling community about who owns a story and who has a right to tell it.

Informal tellers will want to take note of these courtesies. If you are repeating a family story, think carefully about other people's feelings and their privacy. Unless, of course, you are telling this as gossip, in which case invading someone else's privacy is the whole point. Make the tale your own by telling it in your own way. One advantage of the movie-camera technique is that this happens automatically because you are filtering the story through your own imagination and coming up with a new composition based on your inner vision.

PREPARING. When you learn a story by hearing it told aloud, you are doing more than picking words up off a page; you are also absorbing the other elements of the telling: the verbal effects of accent, tone, pitch, and volume, and the nonverbal aspects of facial expression, gesture, and body language. Don't try to remember the story, but concentrate with your listening skills, and see the story in your mind.

If I am retelling a story spontaneously, as when I repeat a joke I heard yesterday, I am simply giving it back as I heard it.

Here is a joke told to me the other day by Jim Albertson, a well-known storyteller and musician from New Jersey. Try it for yourself. Read the joke aloud to yourself and then retell it immediately to a partner, using the movie-camera technique. People who claim they have difficulty remembering jokes often find it a great help to use the storyteller's technique of "seeing" the joke unfolding on their inner movie screen.

Endangered Species

A fellow was hauled into court for shooting a falcon, which, as you know, is an endangered species. The judge threatened to throw the book at him, but the man threw himself on the mercy of the court.

"Listen, Judge, there were some extenuating circumstances

here. I was out in the woods hunting, and I fell down and hurt my leg. I hadn't brought any food with me. All I had was my gun. I lay there for seven days, weak with hunger. Then this bird flew over. I shot it and ate it, and that gave me the strength to walk on out of there. If it hadn't been for that bird, I'd be a dead man today."

The judge was moved to tears. "Those *are* extenuating circumstances," he admitted. "So I reverse my decision. You are free to go."

"Thanks, Judge," the man said.

As he was walking out, the judge added, "By the way, I've always wondered, what does a falcon taste like?"

The man thought a moment and said, "Well, Judge, it's a little hard to describe. I'd say it's about halfway between a California condor and a bald eagle."

Jokes are sort of the fast-food version of storytelling, but their brevity makes them fun to retell and pass around. Jokes are a mystery—who makes these things up? They are circulated by word of mouth, with astonishing speed, as many folklorists have proven.

Tapes and Records

Many libraries have a selection of records and tapes. Some books on tape are excellent, especially when they are read by the author. There are many worthwhile storytelling tapes available through NAPPS, and other sources as well. You can order them from the catalogues listed in the Resources section. I prepare stories from tapes and records exactly the way I would prepare stories borrowed from other tellers. Recorded stories leave me at something of a disadvantage because the teller is not physically present. On the other hand, I can ask the teller on tape to go back and repeat himself as many times as I like, and he will never complain.

If you don't have a tape player in the car, it's well worth the price. While you are driving, you can be learning new stories. I find that if I just leave my tape running as I drive, I spontaneously learn through osmosis. When our family is packing for a long car trip, I always make sure that we have a good batch of storytelling tapes to make the miles roll a little faster.

Written Sources

Much of our spoken lore today has died out and been replaced by written word, so that is what we have to work with. Most of the storytellers working today are what folklorists call revivalists, or people who take stories from secondary sources, usually books, and translate them back into the spoken word.

The oral tradition is indeed very fragile. If a few generations fail to pass along their tales, the chain is broken and the tradition dies out. It is fortunate, in a way, that some people did commit their tales to writing, so we have access to them today. Written material is one of the sources I use most often, both for my work and for storytelling in our family.

LOCATING. The written sources you may want to use for stories could be right on your bookshelf at home. Go through your kids' books to find stories you would like to retell. The library is, of course, another valuable resource.

When working with the written word, I feel it is very important to read the stories aloud. Reading aloud, a close cousin of story-telling, is a great way to ease your way into storytelling. When you have the printed page before you, you can enjoy the spoken word without feeling concerned about forgetting the story. Check Jim Trelease's *Read Aloud Handbook* for solid advice on the art of reading aloud as well as an annotated bibliography of read-aloud books.

My series of historical novels, the Bread Sister Trilogy, is based on the idea of reading aloud for fifteen minutes a night. Many parents have told me that this is the perfect amount of time for their elementary-school-age children. One parent who had read my books had this idea: "When I am reading to the kids at night, I like to sit on the floor in the hallway outside their rooms. The kids lie in bed with their bedroom doors open, and even though they can't see me, they can hear me really well. This way they are not always bugging me to show them the pictures in the book, and I know they are forming pictures in their minds. Besides, the acoustics in the stairwell make my voice sound great!"

As good as reading aloud is, it is not the same as storytelling. When you are reading a story to your kids, you are sticking fairly close to the text. And the kids are picturing the story in the inner world, so there is definitely story-listening taking place. But the important difference is that when you adapt a story from the written form, you filter it through your own psyche. Your own prejudices, values, and ideas interact with the story.

SELECTING. Choosing stories to tell is a crucially important process. The selection of material is the storyteller's signature. Never tell a tale you don't like. Pick one that has some meaning for you. Identify your "hooks," the things in stories that have meaning for you.

Not all tales are tellable. Some stories do not translate well into the spoken form. To be safe, choose written material that has itself come from the spoken form. Folktales and fairy tales are examples of this type of material.

A wonderful source for selecting tellable tales is *The Storyteller's Sourcebook* by Margaret Read MacDonald. This hefty reference tool can save you hours of time in the card catalogue file. MacDonald lists nearly a thousand tellable tales that are available in children's collections. Your local library should have a good number of these. The organization of the sourcebook can help you find variants of tales so that you can recompose a story of your own from several different versions. Stories are listed by subject, by ethnic or geographical area, and by folktale motif.

PREPARING. As you prepare stories to tell, you may wish to edit them. You probably want the stories you tell your children to be consistent with the values you want to pass along. Written material brings you face to face with issues like violence, sexuality, racism, sexism, ageism, and speciesism. Let's take a brief look at the most important issues. Because each of these deserves a long discussion, with equal time given to a variety of viewpoints, I will give several sources you can look up if you want to pursue the fascinating controversy. Then you can come to your own conclusion.

Violence. Many of the tales you will encounter involve a great deal of violence. Bruno Bettelheim, in *The Uses of Enchantment,* points out that dragon-slaying and witch-burning serve an important function. Fairy tales prepare children for life in the real world by providing them inner dragons to slay so that they won't vent their aggressions in the outer world. Bettelheim argues that editing violence out of stories is actually robbing our children of these valuable socialization tools. I do edit out some violence, though, to make the story age-appropriate for my listeners.

I do not deny that we have violent impulses in us and that we must acknowledge them. Stories can indeed help us do just that. In his book *A Little Book on the Human Shadow,* the poet Robert Bly offers an excellent discussion of how stories help us befriend and integrate the dark, repressed, and rejected parts of ourselves that linger in the psyche and cause us to project our own darkness onto other people. A chilling account of the role of evil in stories appears in Marie-Louise von Franz's *Shadow and Evil in Fairy Tales.*

I recommend moderation when telling children stories with violent scenes. Let Gretel push the witch into the oven, but don't dwell on the smell of her burning skin, the sound of her agonized screams, or the sight of the charred corpse.

Sexuality. Sex is a big part of life, and life itself would be impossible without it. So it has a place in our stories. As with violence, I think the key is to be age-appropriate. If you haven't yet taken the plunge with your kids and told them about "the birds and the bees," they aren't going to understand a lot of what goes on in many of the stories they hear.

My wife and I have tried to be pretty open with our own kids about this. One thing that our parents' generation did give us was a more open attitude toward sex, something they didn't have when they were growing up. As George Burns says, "It's hard to keep up with the times. I remember when the air was clean and sex was dirty."

Some acknowledgment of how we handle our sexuality is important. For instance, it will be difficult to do justice to some of the Greek myths unless you approach the concept of rape explicitly. When Hades rapes Persephone and takes her to the underworld, you can't edit that detail out; it's crucial to the story.

Sexism. The stories of Western culture are often sexist. I disagree with those modern tellers who change the old stories. If your princesses must wield swords and say no to their princes, maybe you should select a different story to tell. The old stories often have deeper layers of meaning that we receive unconsciously. Changing the male and female roles short-circuits the insights the tale was meant to convey.

As Robert Bly points out in his excellent tape *Fairy Tales for Men and Women,* the characters in these stories are not people like ourselves. All of the characters within a tale exist within the psyche of one person. The man and woman who get married in the story are really the man and woman inside each one of us joining together and working in harmony.

Thanks to the work of several feminist writers, we now have available stories from traditions all over the world that honor the feminine in both men and women. We may now select from a broader range of tales and offer our daughters a variety of role models to choose from. These stories are also important for our sons as they seek to make contact with the female in their own inner worlds. Merlin Stone's *When God Was a Woman,* Riane Eisler's *The Chalice and the Blade,* and Jean Shinoda Bolen's *Goddesses in Everywoman* are excellent resources for preparing this type of material. Marie-Louise von Franz offers her fresh and original thoughts in *The Feminine in Fairy Tales.*

The women's movement has spawned a parallel men's movement that aims to help men regain what they themselves have lost as a result of the abuses of the patriarchy. Robert Bly is a major force in this movement. His books, tapes, and workshops have helped men address their grief about the present relations of men and women. Bly's work aims to restore men to their true power. Other resources on this subject include the publication *Inroads,* and Bill Moyers's video *A Gathering of Men.*

Racism. Be alert to your own ethnocentrism. My son and I were recently reading an adventure story about some explorers who had gone into the Amazon rainforest to find ancient stone sculptures so they could "donate them to a museum." When the hero's riverboat was attacked by indigenous people with bows and arrows, the explorers opened up with their rifles "to fight off the natives."

I felt it was necessary for me to stop and make an editorial comment. I pointed out that the explorers were invading the local people's terrain for the purpose of stealing their artwork. Supposedly the idea of donating the art objects to a museum gave them the right to do this. I pointed out the unfairness of this. I said that the United States would not send a bunch of explorers to Italy to rip off Michelangelo's statue *David* so we could have it for our museums.

This is a pretty obvious example, but racism creeps into our stories in subtle ways. These abuses are all based on the idea that our lifestyle is the only one worth living and that if we could make everyone else like us, the world would be straightened out. Of course, it is the diversity of the human community that makes life on this planet what it is. It's the same as in the natural world: it wouldn't be much of a planet with nothing but maple trees. One tactic is to search out stories that celebrate the diversity of human life.

Ageism. In the stories of our youth-obsessed culture, old people often seem to appear as witches or wise old men and women or supporting characters for the young lead players. Many of the stories we have are about tasks of the first part of life—about growing up, separating from parents, and finding a marriage partner.

The best book I've seen that addresses stories of later life is *In the Ever After* by Allan B. Chinen. The author recounts traditional tales from all over the world that embody a balanced view of the pains and rewards of the second half of life.

Speciesism. People in our world have only lately begun acknowledging the assumptions we make about the human race's right to dictate what life will be like for other life forms on the planet. Environmental impact statements indicate that other life forms should have their own voices, so to speak. Stories from tribal cultures all over the world reiterate this theme again and again: all life is interconnected, and humans are only one of the many forms that manifest life. An example of this all-embracing perspective shows up in the many stories about humans changing into animals and animals changing into humans. A great collection of these stories appears in *The Language of the Birds*, edited by David Guss. For an eloquent and penetrating discussion of the consequences of contemporary speciesism, see Thomas Berry's *Dream of the Earth*. The author, a Passionist priest who refers to himself as a "geologian," predicts that this recognition of our relationships to the other life forms will lead us humans to the next evolutionary step: redefining the human race on a species level. For a more traditional view, see *Who Speaks for Wolf* by Paula Underwood Spencer. The author, a Seneca writer and teacher, uses a traditional Indian story as a way of suggesting a negotiation process that can take place between humans and the land.

FINAL SCRIPTING. When we work with written material we must base our inner film clip on what is written down. The written word does not always transfer smoothly into the spoken word, though, so we must introduce a scripting step. Scripting involves recomposing the written story into a kind of movie script. When we make our inner movie, we may use this movie script version as our starting place.

First of all, read the story in its written form aloud, speaking the characters' lines and exploring what works and what doesn't. Eliminate the boring parts and beef up the interesting parts. Ascertain why this story attracted you. I heard a storytelling tape one morning, Doug Elliot's *A Raccoon and a Possum*, and was especially attracted to a story about a boy who gets lost in the woods and uses his hunting horn to call his dogs. Since I have been lost in the woods on occasion, I felt a deep sense of resonance with the boy's feelings of despair and hopelessness. His rescue by the dogs comes as a welcome resolution. So that was what hooked me in. If you find a story that evokes this kind of response from you, you will be able to communicate it to your listeners. By the same token, if a story doesn't interest you, how can you expect your listeners to be excited by it? After the initial read-aloud, break the story down into parts and work on story structure. Mark off the invitation, beginning, middle, and end of the story, and keep the tale well proportioned.

Draw a story map, or make an outline in order to clearly follow

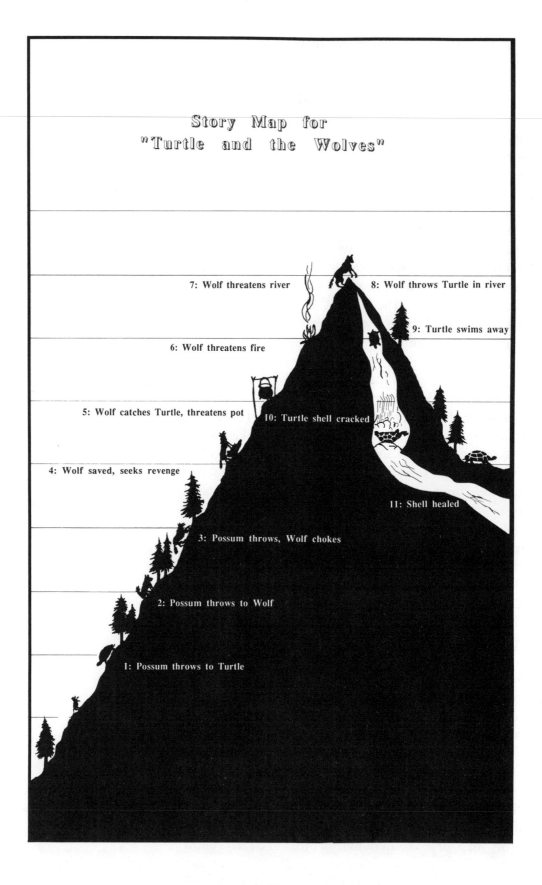

Story Map for
"Turtle and the Wolves"

7: Wolf threatens river

8: Wolf throws Turtle in river

9: Turtle swims away

6: Wolf threatens fire

5: Wolf catches Turtle, threatens pot

10: Turtle shell cracked

4: Wolf saved, seeks revenge

11: Shell healed

3: Possum throws, Wolf chokes

2: Possum throws to Wolf

1: Possum throws to Turtle

the events of the plot. My story maps are drawn like a range of mountains seen from the side, with peaks and valleys to indicate the rising and falling of tension in the story. The story map on page 84 is for the turtle story. A story map helps you to make sure there is a good balance between narration, dialogue, and action in the story. The narrator normally carries the tale at the beginning and at the end; the characters carry the story through its middle. The outline and story map can also help you keep track of the numerology of your story. Think in threes. Possum throws three persimmons down; wolf threatens turtle three times.

Streamline the story. Cut out all the unnecessary description. The listener's imagination will fill in the details. Make every phrase count. Every sentence should economically carry the story forward toward its conclusion. As John Haag, my college writing teacher, said, "If you tell the reader that there is a shotgun hanging over the fireplace, that gun had better go off by the end of the story." Make any judicious editorial changes you wish during the scripting process.

Finally you will be ready to see your script to make an inner movie. In order to get a clear idea of how the scripting process works, let's go back and look at the original version of the turtle and wolf story. This is a Cherokee Indian story published by the ethnologist James Mooney in his *Myths of the Cherokee,* which appeared in the nineteenth annual report of the American Bureau of Ethnology, 1897. It was later adapted as a children's storybook by Corydon Bell called *John Rattling Gourd of Big Cove,* which was a book my father read me as a boy. Here's the story as it appears in Mooney's manuscript.

The Terrapin's Escape from the Wolves

The Possum and the Terrapin went out together to hunt for persimmons and found a tree of ripe fruit. The possum climbed it and was throwing down the persimmons to Terrapin when a Wolf came up and began to snap at the persimmons as they fell, before the Terrapin could reach them.

The possum waited his chance, and at last managed to throw down a large one (some say a bone which he carried with him), so that it lodged in the wolf's throat as he jumped up and choked to death.

"I'll take his ears for hominy spoons," said Terrapin, and cut off the Wolf's ears and started home with them, leaving the Possum still eating persimmons up in the tree. After a while he came to a house and was invited to have some Kanahena gruel from the jar that was set always outside the door.

He sat down beside that jar and dipped up the gruel with one of the Wolf's ears for a spoon. The people noticed and wondered. When he was satisfied he went on, but soon came to another house and was asked to have some more Kanahena. He dipped it up again with the Wolf's ear and went on when he had enough.

Soon the news went around that the Terrapin had killed the Wolf and was using this ears for spoons. All the wolves got together and followed the Terrapin's trail until they came up with him and made him prisoner. Then they held a council to decide what to do with him, and agreed to boil him in a clay pot.

They brought in a pot but Terrapin only laughed at it and said that if they put him into that thing he would kick it all to pieces. They said they would burn him in the fire, but the Terrapin laughed again and said he would put it out. Then they decided to throw him in the deepest hole in the river and drown him. The Terrapin begged and prayed them not to do it, but they paid no attention, and dragged him over to the river and threw him in. That was just what the Terrapin had been waiting for all the time, and he dived under the water and came up on the other side and got away.

Some say that when he was thrown in the river he struck against a rock, which broke his back in a dozen places. He sang a medicine song:

Gu daye wu, Gu daye wu
(I have sewed myself together, I have sewed myself together.)

And the pieces came together. But the scars remain on his shell to this day.

Now go back and read my adaptation of the story as it appears on pages 37–39.

Many of the issues we have discussed come up in the adapting of this story for telling. One thing to keep in mind is that there is no one way to adapt it; there will be as many different versions of the story as there are storytellers. In the end, each of these things is a judgment call. When we went through this story focusing on outer tools, I stressed that there were many ways of telling it. Simply use this as a guide. You may disagree with my choices, and that's fine. I'll be asking you to script up your own version.

Let me call your attention to some of the major changes I made to the story along with my reasons for doing so.

In the opening lines of the story, the narrator uses asides to offer three additional pieces of information. The first is that a persimmon is a sticky fruit. You must be careful not to assume that kids know this. The second is that this was in the days when animals could talk. This phrase places the story for the listeners, letting them know that it is not a true-life animal story, but one that takes place in the mythical past. The third points out that this was in the days when the turtle's shell was "smooth and shining." Otherwise, listeners would naturally assume that the turtle's shell had always been cracked.

Note that while the narrative and the attributions are in the past tense, the characters' lines are spoken in the present tense. This device brings us closer to the characters. In Mooney's version, by contrast, much of the dialogue is paraphrased. It is more exciting when the characters speak for themselves. When their words are filtered through the narrator, we get the sense that we are being told about the story rather than being told the story.

Instead of killing the wolf off in the early part of the story, I kept him alive. This not only softened the brutality of the tale but allowed me to use him in the second half of the story. Of course, you could take the other route and describe the wolf's choking in graphic detail. But what would be the point? This is a humorous animal story. Save the gruesome stuff for ghost stories on Halloween.

In the original version, the turtle cuts off the wolf's ears for soup spoons. Sometimes I put this in and sometimes I leave it out, depending on my audience. When I told this version to my own kids, they accepted it very naturally and didn't think any more about it. Other kids became so intent on the mutilation motif that they didn't hear the rest of the story.

Many stories have a "kicker" at the end. In this one, it is the detail about the turtle hitting the rock and cracking his shell. The story could have ended with the turtle swimming away unharmed, but this would not be nearly as satisfying.

As you can see, I followed Mooney's version pretty closely. But that is only one approach. If you find a story you like, you can use a reference work like *The Storyteller's Sourcebook* to find variants of the tale. After reading several versions, you can recompose the elements you like best into a new adaptation. I did this with my story "Dark Catrina," which appears on my recording *When the Moon Is Full: Supernatural Stories from the Pennsylva-*

nia Mountains. It is a story about witchcraft and wolf hunting that I assembled from several traditional mountain motifs.

In the story of the silver lake trout, I combined a traditional tall tale with boyhood memories of my real-life grandfather. Here is a version of the tale of the walking fish from *Botkin's Treasury of American Folklore* by Andrew Botkin. You might have fun comparing this with my story, which appears in the introduction to this book.

The Walking Fish

Once there was a half-breed Indian who had a pet trout named Tommy, which he kept in a barrel. But the trout got pretty big and had to have the water changed a good deal to keep him alive. The Indian was too lazy to do that and thought he would teach the trout to live out of water. So he did.

He commenced by taking Tommy out of the barrel for a few moments at a time, pretty often, and then he took him out oftener and kept him out longer, and by and by Tommy got so he could stay out a good while if he was in the wet grass. Then the Indian found he could leave him in the wet grass all night and pretty soon that trout could live in the shade whether the grass was wet or not.

By that time he had got pretty tame too and he would follow the Indian around a good deal, and when the Indian would go out to dig worms for him, Tommy would go along and pick up the worms for himself. The Indian thought everything of that fish, and when Tommy got so he didn't need water at all, but could go anywhere—down the dusty road and stay all day in the hot sun—you never saw the Indian without his trout. Show people wanted to buy Tommy but the Indian said he wouldn't sell a fish like that for any money. You'd see him coming to town with Tommy following along in the road behind, just like a dog, only of course it traveled a good deal like a snake, and most as fast.

Well, it was pretty sad the way that Indian lost his trout, and it was curious too. He started for town one day, with Tommy coming behind, as usual. There was a bridge in the road and when the Indian came to it he saw there was a plank off, but he went on over it without thinking. By and by he looked around for Tommy and Tommy wasn't there. He went back a ways and called, but he couldn't see anything of his pet. Then he came to the bridge and saw the hole, and thought right away that maybe his trout had got in there. So he went to the hole and looked down, and sure enough, there was Tommy, floating up on the water, bottom side up. He'd tumbled through that hole into the brook and drowned.

You now have read about the tools and basic skills you need to create your own tales. The next chapter contains story-related activities that will help you explore your imagination further as you master the storyteller's tools.

CHAPTER 4

In the final two chapters of this book we will undertake voyages that give us a clearer understanding of the two basic building blocks of stories: time and space. The storyteller's skill is to alter our perception so that we can experience dimensions of time and space that are not available to us in normal waking hours. With stories we can go outside of normal linear time to travel into the past and future; through storytelling, we can also explore inner space—the landscape of the imagination, which is not visible in the outer world.

In this chapter we will:

- Inquire into the nature of time itself and learn to work with time.
- Learn how to alter our listeners' perception of time, speeding time up and slowing it down, moving backward and forward through time, and viewing time from a nonhuman perspective.
- Use the TimeRopes approach to gain a new understanding of time and our place in it.

Voyaging Through Time

WHAT IS TIME?

We all know intuitively that time is one of the most basic forces in our lives, but talking about it doesn't help us understand it. As soon as we try to discuss time, we get lost. In his discourse on the nature of time, Saint Augustine put it this way: "If no one asks me, I know what it is. If I wish to explain it to him who asks, I do not know." Isaac Newton thought he understood time when he declared in 1687: "Time flows equally without relation to anything external." In 1905, a young Swiss scientist named Albert Einstein stated that time was not constant, but relative. My favorite definition of time is one I saw scrawled on a men's room wall when I was in college: "Time is nature's way of keeping everything from happening at once."

If you want to stretch your cognitive powers, read *Time's Arrows* by Richard Morris and *A Brief History of Time* by Stephen W. Hawking. Many of the ideas for the voyages we will take in this chapter come from those books.

Gernot Winkler, Director of Time Services at the U.S. Naval Observatory in Washington, D.C., notes, "We have given more attention to measuring time than to anything in nature. But time remains an abstraction, a riddle that exists only in our minds." Is time an abstraction? It strikes me that the only way to get a grasp on time is to do it literally, to find a physical way of handling and manipulating time. That's why I dreamed up a process that I call the TimeRopes approach. In this chapter, I will show how to construct TimeRopes and use them to take voyages into time.

TIMEROPES

About five years ago, when I was giving "Living History" presentations in the public schools, I became frustrated with the very idea of history. I wanted to impress on students that recorded history encompasses only a small percentage of the total time humans have lived on this planet, and only an infinitesimal percentage of the lifespan of the earth itself.

Then I came across a wonderful book called *Timescale: An Atlas of the Fourth Dimension* by Nigel Calder. *Timescale* is basically a long time line, with every event from the Big Bang to the invention of the reusable spaceship clearly marked. I wanted to share Calder's idea with the students in a physical, immediate way. Most of the information included on my TimeRopes is taken directly from Calder's book.

My first thought was to make a long strip of paper, like a ticker tape, that could be stretched across the room. But I didn't have any ticker tape. I did, however, have some rope. I have always had a real affection for rope, and we have a lot of rope around the house. So I started making TimeRopes.

The first TimeRopes I used in the schools were twenty and thirty feet long, of quarter-inch manila rope, with the events along the time line marked by colored ribbons. These ropes proved to be a very effective visual way of putting events into perspective in time. My TimeRopes are constructed using the history of the universe that has been developed by the Western scientific tradition. We might also make TimeRopes representing history according to the biblical tradition, for instance. TimeRopes can be used to make time lines of our lives so we can see the events of our lives clearly represented in visual form.

As storytellers, we will be working with four types of time:

- Total Time—from the beginning to the end of time itself
- Planet Time—from the formation of the earth to the present
- Human Time—from the appearance of the first humans to the present
- Life Time—from birth to death in an individual's life

What we call clock time, incidentally, is a fairly recent phenomenon. The first clocks didn't come into use until around 1345, and those weren't very accurate.

DOING TIME

Use the charts on pages 94–95 as your guides in constructing the ropes. All the measurements have been worked out so you can simply copy them. Note that the scale given with each chart allows you to easily transfer the events from the chart to your TimeRope. For example, your "Total TimeRope" will be 120 inches long, representing 60 billion years. The scale of your rope will be 2 inches = one billion years.

For your lifeline, you can make your own chart, similar to the sample chart showing my own life up to my present age.

Here are the materials you will need to make your TimeRopes:

- Approximately 10 feet of rope for each TimeRope. The ideal rope is a thin, strong cord like the kind used to operate window blinds. This cord is available in 50-foot rolls at the hardware store. Whatever kind of rope you choose, it should be one that can be easily marked with a colored marking pen.
- About 100 twist ties. Get a variety of colors if you can.
- Colored marking pens
- A yardstick or ruler

If you want more flamboyant TimeRopes, you can use twisted or braided rope and colored ribbons. The ribbons can be easily attached by twisting the lay of the rope against itself and inserting the ribbons between the strands. It can be fun for kids to string these colorful ropes around the house like cosmic clotheslines.

To construct the TimeRopes:

1. Select a workplace. The ideal spot is a room where you can lay out the full length of the ropes. You may want to spread newspapers on the floor.

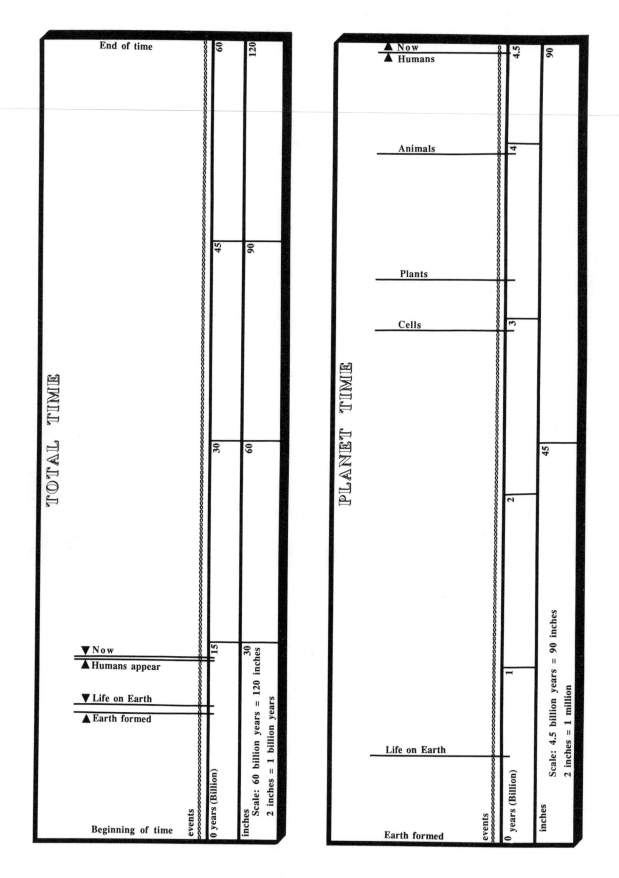

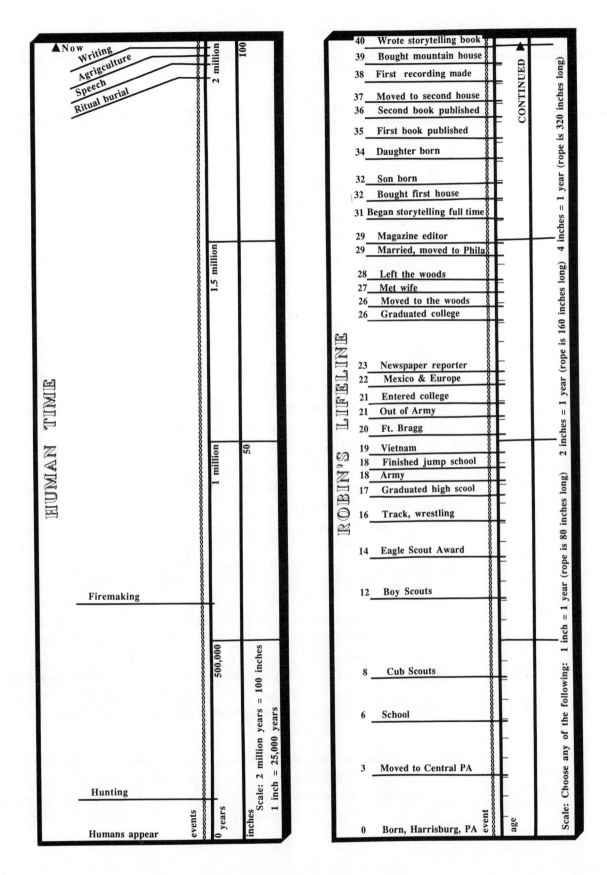

HUMAN TIME

▲ Now
Writing
Agrigculture
Speech
Ritual burial

2 million
100

1.5 million

1 million
50

500,000

Firemaking

Hunting

Humans appear

events
0 years
inches

Scale: 2 million years = 100 inches
1 inch = 25,000 years

ROBIN'S LIFELINE

40	Wrote storytelling book
39	Bought mountain house
38	First recording made
37	Moved to second house
36	Second book published
35	First book published
34	Daughter born
32	Son born
32	Bought first house
31	Began storytelling full time
29	Magazine editor
29	Married, moved to Phila
28	Left the woods
27	Met wife
26	Moved to the woods
26	Graduated college
23	Newspaper reporter
22	Mexico & Europe
21	Entered college
21	Out of Army
20	Ft. Bragg
19	Vietnam
18	Finished jump school
18	Army
17	Graduated high scool
16	Track, wrestling
14	Eagle Scout Award
12	Boy Scouts
8	Cub Scouts
6	School
3	Moved to Central PA
0	Born, Harrisburg, PA

CONTINUED

event   age

Scale: Choose any of the following: 1 inch = 1 year (rope is 80 inches long)   2 inches = 1 year (rope is 160 inches long)   4 inches = 1 year (rope is 320 inches long)

2. Cut the rope into lengths, following the measurements given on the chart. Remember to allow an extra 2 feet on each end of the rope so you have something to hold on to.

3. Mark the ropes. The measurements in all of the diagrams are given in inches. Leave the first 2 feet of the rope unmarked, then begin to mark the scale, using a colored marking pen. At the other end of the rope, leave the last 2 feet unmarked. (The Total TimeRope, for instance, requires 10 feet of rope, so you'll need 14 feet of rope all together: 10 feet plus 2 feet at each end.)

   To speed up the process of marking the scale, lay the yardstick beside the rope and use it as a sight guide. Put a mark on the rope at each 1-inch interval. Using a different color for the foot demarcations will make the scale easier to read.

   When you have completed the first rope, use it as a template. Lay it beside the other ropes and mark them all at once. Keep the ropes taut as you work; tie them to the ends of chair legs.

4. Using the chart as a guide, fasten the twist ties firmly around the rope to mark the events.

5. Add the finishing touches. Wrap the two extra feet at either end of the rope with tape or color these parts of the rope with a marker to separate them visually from the time line itself.

6. Making the Life TimeRope requires an additional step. You must create the diagram of events yourself. The life time line may be crowded with events, so you may want to create a key and mark the events with numbers on your diagram. To make the personal life line itself, plot out the major events of your life from birth to now on your chart. Once you are satisfied with your chart, you are ready to make your personal TimeRope. Just as you did with the other ropes, use the chart to transfer the events from paper to rope. Note that I have given you a choice of three scales to follow, depending upon how long you would like your Life TimeRope to be.

One woman said, "It took us days to make up the diagrams for our life lines. We spent a lot of time talking about the important events in our personal and family lives. The kids got a clearer sense of the things that have happened in our family's various moves and changes, and we talked for the first time about our differing perspectives on things that have happened."

Observe your tendency to record outer events, but do not neglect inner events. Use different colored markers or twist ties to record inner world events. Can you pinpoint the moment at which you became an adult? When did you first realize that you had to support yourself?

Ask your children questions to help them identify the crucial events in their lives. *A Journey through Your Childhood: A Write-in Guide for Reliving Your Past*, by Christopher Biffle, and *Where Do I Go from Here with My Life?* by John Crystal and Richard Bolles, are two books that can help.

Note that the life line diagram assumes a lifetime of about eighty years. You may wish to set up your time lines for a lifetime of one hundred.

VOYAGING WITH TIMEROPES

We are ready to use our ropes for a variety of imaginative voyages. I hope that the ones I have outlined in this book will inspire you to devise your own voyages.

TIME: 10 minutes

GOAL: To experience the vastness and the bounty of time.

PREPARATION: Prepare the room with the Total Time-Rope and drawing materials. Position the TimeRope so you can see its entire length at a glance. Stretch the rope between two chairs, or two trees outside, or lay it flat on the floor. To make the rope easier to read, write the name of each event on a piece of paper, and place it on the floor underneath the marker on the rope.

INSTRUCTIONS:

- "Let's begin our voyages through total time by sitting with eyes open and voyaging down the time line from beginning to end."

- "Some scientists think that time has a beginning and an end. Time began when a huge explosion created the universe, and the universe began to expand. Time will stop when the motion of the explosion stops and everything becomes still. They don't know for sure when this

VOYAGE 10

Total Time

will happen; it will probably be fifty billion or sixty billion years before time stops."

- "Let's look at the time line to see the events we have marked on it. The first mark represents the beginning of time, when the universe was created by a big bang or explosion that started objects moving outward through space. The second mark represents the formation of the earth, four and a half billion years ago. Life came to earth half a billion years later, and humans only two million years ago. We don't have a mark small enough on this time line to show the tiny bit of time that humans have lived on earth."

- "Look at the mark for the present time, thirteen and a half billion years since the beginning of time. We have come about a quarter of the way through total time. This mark at the end of the time line shows where time ends, sixty billion years from the beginning of time."

- "Let's close our eyes now and take a voyage through total time."

- "With eyes closed, go into the imagination." (Pause)

- "See yourself high up in the air, looking down on the Total TimeRope as if it were a straight river in the landscape far below. Imagine that you can fly along the length of the rope, looking down and observing events as they occur."

- "Begin by looking down at the beginning of time on the rope. See the big explosion that created the universe." (Pause)

- "See the gases swirling in space like a thick fog."

- "See the fog clearing and the stars forming into groups called galaxies. See planets circling the stars."

- "See our own home planet, the earth, forming as it circles our star, the sun."

- "See the surface of the earth cooling and the oceans forming."

- "See the first bits of life swimming in the ocean, wiggly little things that will grow into bigger, more complex forms of life."

- "See animals coming to the earth and growing into a huge celebration of life. See them fly, swim, crawl, and run."

- "See the first humans coming into the world."

- "See the present moment of time."
- "Take a few moments to fly ahead into the future. Go to the end of time and see what happens. Take about five minutes to do that now. When you have come to the end of time, wait there in the stillness until I call you back. Let's voyage ahead now, into the future." (5-minute pause)
- "Now that we have come to the end of time, let's turn around and return to the beginning of time, flying quickly over the length of the rope."
- "Go through the events on the TimeRope one more time, but this time, imagine that you *are* the TimeRope. You are time itself. You feel the events happening inside you, or on you, or within you. See how it feels, going through Total Time from beginning to end, not as an observer, but as time itself. When you reach the end of time, stop, and wait there in the stillness to be called back." (5-minute pause)
- "Now that we have explored the end of time, come back into yourself and fly back to the beginning of time."

- "We are going to climb out of imagination now, and back into the room. Keep your eyes closed. Rub your hands together. Rub your face. When you are ready, open your eyes and come back into the room."
- "If you wish, you may silently take paper and drawing materials and make an illustration of your voyage."
- "If you wish, you may tell the story of your voyage."
- "The voyage is now complete."

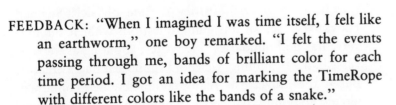

FEEDBACK: "When I imagined I was time itself, I felt like an earthworm," one boy remarked. "I felt the events passing through me, bands of brilliant color for each time period. I got an idea for marking the TimeRope with different colors like the bands of a snake."

A mother said, "I felt a sense of relief when I went to the end of time. I saw that it doesn't end permanently, it just starts all over again."

FOLLOW-UP TO VOYAGE 10: Time is such an important presence in our lives that it is hard to imagine it as having a beginning and an end. Richard Morris, the author of *Time's Arrows,* says "The Big Bang may have been the beginning of time. In this case, the question 'What happened before the Big Bang?' would be meaningless; there would be no such thing as 'before.' " About the end of time, Morris says:

> If the universe is closed, there may be not only a beginning but also an end of time. A closed universe must eventually collapse upon itself. Since it appears that the universe will continue expanding for some time yet, a closed universe would not begin to contract for at least another forty or fifty billion years.
>
> If the universe did indeed begin as a bubble of space-time in a primordial chaos, the big crunch might cause it to return to the original chaos from which it came.

If, on the other hand, the universe is open, space will continue to expand until stars and planets collapse into black holes, matter will decay into smaller and smaller particles, and even the energy in visible light, X-rays, and ultraviolet radiation will dissipate.

"As the universe becomes emptier and emptier," Morris writes, "as it evaporates into nothing, events will cease to take place. Without events to mark its passing, time cannot be measured, or even defined."

Delving into the nature of time can cause kids to ask some very interesting questions. As we adults attempt to answer their questions, it is reassuring to note that even the greatest scientific minds have been able to do no more than create interesting scenarios about time. You might have fun creating your own scenarios about the birth and death of time.

In his book *A Brief History of Time*, physicist Stephen Hawking poses an intriguing question: what if the universe has no boundaries? He writes, "So long as the universe had a beginning, we could suppose it had a creator. But if the universe is really completely self-contained, having no boundary or edge, it would have neither beginning nor end: it would simply be. What place, then, for a creator?"

Flying over the Total TimeRope gives us some extra-human views of time. Shifting to the perspective of time itself helps us to leave behind the claustrophobic notions we humans hold about time.

TIME: 10 minutes

VOYAGE 11

Planet Time

GOAL: To look closely at the events that have taken place during the lifetime of the earth, and to experience time from the perspective of the planet as a whole.

PREPARATION: Stretch the Planet TimeRope out on the floor. Stretch the Total TimeRope out beside it. Seat the family to review the events marked on the rope. Have blindfolds and art materials on hand.

INSTRUCTIONS:

- "Let's sit quietly and look at the Planet TimeRope. This rope represents the life of the planet so far, four and a half billion years."

- "Notice where the lifeline of the planet fits into Total Time. The Total TimeRope spans sixty billion years; the planet TimeRope, four and a half billion years."

- "Let's travel through Planet Time now, noting the events that take place."

- "Planet time begins when the earth was formed. The first life on the planet appeared in the seas four billion years ago. Life became more and more complex. Plants developed 1,300 million years ago, animals 670 million years ago. Humans appeared a mere two million years ago."

- "Close your eyes now and fly over the Planet TimeRope as an observer, watching the events that have taken place from the formation of the earth until the present moment. As you fly along, feel free to dip down toward the TimeRope to look more closely at the events as they occur. I'll give you about three minutes to make this voyage. When you reach the present moment, simply wait there until I call you back. Let's make our voyage through Planet Time now." (3-minute pause)

- "Return now to the beginning of Planet Time. You will now travel through the earth's events again, but this time you will *be* the earth, and feel those events taking place within you, and upon you, and around you, and in your atmosphere. Pay special attention to how it feels to be the earth."

- "I'll give you about three minutes to feel yourself evolving from the time when you were a lump of molten rock whirling up in space up to the present moment, when you are a green planet bursting with flowers, ocean life, animals, people, thunderstorms, and birds. When you reach the present moment, simply wait there until I call you back. Let's travel, please." (3-minute pause)
- "Come back into yourself now, and fly back to the beginning of Planet Time."
- "Come out of imagination and back into the room."
- "Keep your eyes closed and rub your hands together. Rub your face, and, when you are ready, open your eyes and come back into the room."
- "If you wish, illustrate your voyage."
- "If you wish, tell about your voyage into planet time."
- "The voyage is now complete."

FEEDBACK: One girl said, "I had trouble imagining what the early animals looked like, so I drew mostly dinosaurs."

A boy said, "I felt as if I was the earth growing up and becoming more mature. It felt sad to have pollution in my atmosphere and to have humans digging into me and cutting down the forests, which I imagined as my hair."

FOLLOW-UP TO VOYAGE 11: For some thoughts and eye-opening photos about the earth as seen from space, read *The Home Planet*, edited by Kevin Kelley. This book contains firsthand accounts from space explorers from all over the world. The photos help our kids dream ahead into the future of the planet. As author Fred Hoyle said in 1948: "Once a photograph of the earth, taken from the outside, is available, a new idea, as powerful as any in history will be let loose."

In an essay in the book *Thinking Like a Mountain*, John Seed and Joanna Macy write:

We have been but recently in human form. If the earth's whole history were compressed into twenty-four hours, Organic life would begin only at 5 P.M., mammals emerge at 11:30, and from amongst them, at only seconds to midnight, our species.

In our long planetary journey we have taken more ancient forms than these we now wear. Some of these forms we remember in our mother's womb, wear vestigal tails and gills, grow fins for hands.

The deep ecology movement gives us a new perspective on the planetary environment. It is espoused by environmental organizations like Earth First!, and it involves considering the planet as a whole, from a nonhuman perspective, and realizing that each life form on earth deserves an equal vote in decisions that will affect the future of the planet.

Thomas Berry notes in his *Dream of the Earth*, though, that if there were ever an actual "continental congress," in which every life form on the continent got one vote, the humans would be kicked out of the community. Berry suggests that the present task humans face is redefining themselves as a species. Our next evolutionary step, he says, must carry us beyond our technological cleverness. It will renew the relationship between humans and the earth.

As the pioneering environmentalist John Muir said, "Most people live on the earth, not in it."

Seeing planet time from the viewpoint of the earth itself helps us to live in the earth.

For insightful discussions about the earth as a whole system, and about passing this image of the earth on to our children, see James Lovelock's *Gaia* and *The Ages of Gaia*.

VOYAGE 12

Human Time

TIME: 10 minutes

GOAL: To review the development of the human species, and to experience a kinship with our human ancestors.

PREPARATION: Stretch the Human TimeRope out beside the Total and Planet TimeRopes. Have art materials and blindfolds on hand.

INSTRUCTIONS:

- "Let's view our Human TimeRope. This rope represents two million years. This period fits into the very end of Planet Time to date."

- "Let's review the events on the Human TimeRope. We begin with the appearance of the original humans two million years ago in Africa. We were apelike creatures at that time. At 1.9 million years ago, we began to hunt to obtain food for ourselves. Fire making, another important skill, developed 1.4 million years ago. One hundred thousand years ago, humans practiced ritual burial, evidence that we were thinking about the afterlife. At forty-five thousand years ago we developed the ability to speak and tell stories. Agriculture first appeared ten thousand years ago. The written word originated five thousand years ago. Since that time, the pace of life has quickened, and the human species has grown to fill the earth. All of what we call history has occurred in the last five thousand years."

- "Let's close our eyes now and fly along the Human Time-Rope as observers, watching the human race grow from its beginning until the present moment. Dip down nearer the rope at any point if you would like a closer look at the events. Take about three minutes to do that. When you arrive at the present moment, simply wait there until I call you back. Let's make our flight now." (3-minute pause)

- "Return now to the beginning of the Human Time-Rope."

- "Now, as you move again through Human Time, experience yourself as the human species itself. Feel yourself evolving from an apelike creature into a modern human. Observe the development of the skills that help humans live as they do today. When you reach the present moment at the end of the Human TimeRope, wait for me to call you back. You'll have about three minutes to make this journey. Let's begin." (3-minute pause)

- "Come back into yourself now, and fly back to the beginning of human time. We will come out of imagination now and back into the room."

- "Keep your eyes closed and rub your hands together. Rub your face, and, when you are ready, open your eyes and come back into the room."

- "If you wish, make an illustration of your voyage."

- "If you wish, tell a story of your explorations into Human Time."

- "The voyage is now complete."

FEEDBACK: "I experienced a lot of pride in the human species," one man said. "It was amazing to feel the changes taking place in me when I imagined myself as the human race. Our species has learned a lot in a short period of time."

FOLLOW-UP TO VOYAGE 12: Inquiries into the beginnings of our species help us to connect with our ancestors and to predict where the human race is headed.

Thomas Berry has suggested that each species adds something unique to the earth. If the humpbacked whales, for instance, should become extinct, the total imagination of the earth would grow poorer. "If we lived on the moon," Berry says, "our imaginations would be as barren as the landscape of the moon. It is the celebratory function of this planet that makes it so unique."

Sister Miriam McGillis, in her audio tape *The Fate of the Earth,* comments, "We are like teenagers now, with incredible powers. The question is, Do we have the wisdom and maturity to use our powers?"

Explorations into our evolution as a species can help us answer this question.

TIME: 10 minutes

GOAL: To view our lives from a new perspective; to note patterns and cycles in them.

PREPARATION: Stretch your Life TimeRope out beside the Total, Planet, and Human TimeRopes. Have art materials and blindfolds available.

INSTRUCTIONS:

- "Let's review our Life TimeRopes now. We'll each describe the events of our lives, from our births to the present."

- "Now you will travel through your life, reliving the experience of each event. You may fly along the rope as you did in other voyages, or, if you prefer, you may simply imagine the events as they happened to you. Take about three minutes now to sit with eyes open and travel along your TimeRope. When you come to the present moment, stop and wait there." (3-minute pause)

- "Return now to the beginning of your life line."

- "Come out of imagination now, into the room."

VOYAGE 13

Life Time

- "Close your eyes, rub your hands together, rub your face, and when you are ready, open your eyes and come back to the room."
- "If you wish, make an illustration of your voyage."
- "If you wish, tell what you discovered as you explored the time of your life."
- "The voyage is now complete."

Story told by African Mother
Molna on son's tenth birthday.
Today Zeppa you become a man. You will join our tribe's hunters. I remember well the day you were born. I was out looking for berries far from our home. I felt it was time for you to be born. I made a nest under a large tree and within a short time something wonderful happened — I met you Zeppa. You make me very proud.

FEEDBACK: "I was very moved to go back into my early life and recover some memories from my very early childhood," one father said.

"I had fun voyaging into the future," a girl noted. "I was a little afraid to go to the end of my life, but I did, and when I died, I became a baby and started all over again."

FOLLOW-UP TO VOYAGE 13: My own family enjoys using our Life TimeRopes in several ways. We have made a family time line by laying our ropes alongside each other with the events matched up. The birthday at the beginning of my son's time line, for example, lines up with the point on my own rope marking his birth. The family time line allows us to see all our lives together. Among other things, this is an easy way to figure out when you are likely to become a grandparent. By measuring ahead on your child's rope, you can see what will be happening in your life at that time. I pictured a huge family reunion, with several generations of TimeRopes lying together, like eels in the ocean.

On birthdays, we review the year that has passed and add additional markers to our ropes. We consider how individual events fit into the larger context of our lives.

I sometimes like to sit and hold a period of my life in my hands. I can hold my college years, for instance, in my palm, and think about what that was, telling a story from that period. This is a great way to fill in the missing years: the time between your birth and your first memory.

We use this rope as a story-starter. Kids can ask to hear a story from a certain point on the lifeline.

You can use the ropes to mark out cycles in your life. By simply holding the rope at arm's length, you can see clusters of events and perhaps long stretches where no major events occurred. How exciting it is for our kids to see that long stretch of unused time ahead of them.

Whenever we deal with time, some sadness comes up, as when we voyage ahead and see our death. Countless religions and philosophies have devoted themselves to allaying this sadness. Your voyage into the lifeline may lead you back further into your own religious or ethnic tradition.

In the following excerpt from *Man and Time,* J. B. Priestly relates a dream:

I was standing on the top of a very high tower, alone, looking down upon myriads of birds flying in one direction; every kind of bird was there, all the birds in the world. It was a noble sight, this vast aerial river of birds.

But now in some mysterious fashion, the gear was changed, and time sped up, so that I saw generations of birds, watched them break their shells, flutter into life, mate, weaken, falter, and die. Wings grew only to crumble; bodies were sleek and then, in a flash, bled and shriveled; and death struck everywhere at a second.

What was the use of all this blind struggle toward life, this eager trying of wings, this hurried mating, this flight and surge, all this gigantic, meaningless biological effort? As I stared down, seeming to see each creature's ignoble little history almost at a glance, I felt sick at heart. It would be better if not one of them, not one of all of us, had been born, if the struggle ceased forever.

I stood on my tower, still alone, desperately unhappy. But now the gear was changed again and time went faster still, and it was rushing by at such a rate, that the birds could not show any movement, but were like an enormous plain, sown with feathers. But along this plain, flickering through the bodies themselves, there now passed a sort of white flame, trembling, dancing, then hurrying on; and as soon as I saw it I knew that this white flame was life itself, the very quintessence of being; and then it came to me, in a rocket-burst of ecstasy, that nothing mattered, nothing could ever matter, because nothing else was real but this quivering and hurrying lambency of beings.

Birds, men, or creatures not yet shaped and colored, all were of no account except so far as this flame of life traveled through them. It left nothing to mourn over behind it; what I had thought as tragedy was mere emptiness or a shadow show; for now all real feeling was caught and purified and danced on ecstatically with the white flame of life.

I had never felt before such deep happiness as I knew at the end of my dream of the tower and the birds.

SUMMARY

Now that you and your family have voyaged beyond the limited, everyday concept of time, you can voyage into time as often as you like, then return to tell your stories.

In the next chapter, we will build on our work with time as we take similar voyages into inner space—into the imagination.

CHAPTER 5

Exploring Inner Space

In this chapter, we will:

- Make an exploratory voyage into the inner landscape and map our route so that we can follow it again on subsequent voyages.
- Make contact with guardian animals that live in this inner landscape, and learn how they can help us.
- Locate the home of our inner storyteller and reestablish our dialogue with this important inner guide.

The focus of each of the voyages we have made to the inner world has been the acquiring of a special skill. In this chapter, though, we aim to explore the inner landscape and make accurate maps of our voyage routes. We will also contact the beings who live in our imagination, humans and animals. The ability to navigate in the inner world is extremely important to the storyteller. The rules and laws that operate in the outer world will not necessarily apply there, so we need to learn new ways of traveling inside. Let's begin by looking at the nature of this inner territory.

In his book *A Little Course in Dreams,* Robert Bosnak writes:

A dream is not a story, not a movie or a text or a theater play. A dream is a happening in space, an articulation of space.

We find ourselves in a space we call "dream" upon awakening. In that space we experience things we can talk about upon awakening as a dream story. But the dream story is not the dream itself. The dream itself is a texture woven of space and time inside which we find ourselves.

Bosnak might be describing our stories as well. We experience the story in the inner world, as an event taking place in the inner landscape. Then we do our best to describe to our listeners what we have seen during our travels in inner space.

VOYAGE 14

Traveling in the Tree

TIME: 20 minutes

GOAL: To make an exploratory voyage into the imagination, tracing the routes we follow.

PREPARATION: Prepare the room. Have blindfolds, paper, and crayons on hand.

INSTRUCTIONS:

- "Lie comfortably on the floor with your blindfold in place, enjoying the silence of the room." (Pause)
- "Go into your imagination now and see a field." (Pause)
- "In the center of the field, see a large tree." (Pause)
- "Walk into the field now and place your hands on the bark of the tree. Take a few moments to get to know your tree, feeling its texture against your skin. Place your cheek against the trunk, breathing in the smells of your tree, or place your ear to the trunk to hear any sounds within the tree. Take a few moments now to experience these things." (Pause)
- "Look down and see that the roots of your tree reach into the ground. Tilt your head back and see that the branches of your tree grow up into the sky and the clouds. It's a good, strong tree."
- "Go into your tree now. Only you yourself will know the right way to enter your tree. You are in imagination now. You are not restricted by the ordinary laws of science. So, in whatever way seems right to you, go into your tree." (Pause)
- "Once inside, take a look around. You are now at the juncture of the paths that lead through your tree. You can move downward into the roots or travel up the trunk into the branches of the tree. You are now at the place from which you can enter and exit your tree."
- "Our first excursion will take us into the roots of your tree, to learn what's down there. You can move about in the tree in whatever way seems best to you. This is your tree."
- "Let's head down the trunk now, inside your tree, into the roots. Take a few moments to explore this area of your tree." (5-minute pause)

- "This will be just a short exploration. Know that you can stay here just as long as you like and return here any time you like. There is much to explore in this area of your tree, and each time you return there will always be more to see and more to learn. For now, let's head back up to the trunk of the tree, to the place where you first entered." (Pause)

- "Now we will travel upward into the branches of your tree. Take a few moments to make a short exploration of the area, to learn what's there for you in the upper portion of your tree. Do that now." (5-minute pause)

- "You can return to this place and continue your travels here whenever you like. For now, though, let's head back down into the tree, to the entrance in the trunk." (Pause)

- "Take a last look around inside your tree. Speak to the tree now. Say whatever you like. You can communicate with your tree with words, gestures, or thoughts. You will exit the tree now the same way you entered it, and go back into your body with your hands on the bark of the tree." (Pause)

- "Look around the field. You can return to the field and to this tree whenever you like."

- "Come out of the field now, out of imagination, and back into your body in the room. Keep your eyes closed, rub your hands together, rub your face, and, when you are ready, open your eyes and come back into the room."

- "Silently take paper and drawing materials and make a map of your voyage, marking your routes within the tree."

- "If you like, tell us about your travels now."

- "The voyage is now complete."

FEEDBACK: "I was easily able to move about in my tree. I made myself small and crawled in through a hole in the bark. I was so small that I could easily travel through the capillary system of the tree, down to the root hairs and all the way up to the uppermost leaves, where I was bathed in green light," one mother said.

Her son remarked, "I just melted into my tree and headed down to the roots. I found worms down there who were using the ends of the roots for telephones.

When I got up to the branches, there was an owl sitting there, listening to what the worms were saying to him."

Another woman said, "My first thought was that this was meant to be my family tree, and when I looked at the tree I saw that it was decayed and dying, which is how I see my family. Then I realized that it doesn't have to be a family tree. It can be a tree connecting me to the earth and sky. When I thought that, the tree became healthy and strong again."

FOLLOW-UP TO VOYAGE 14: The image of the tree as a vessel for traveling in the inner world dates back into primitive times. In his book *Dreamtime and Inner Space,* Holger Kalweit writes, "The World Tree—the *axis mundi* connecting heaven, earth, and the underworld—is seen as an opening or channel into other realms of being. Along it, gods and beings of the beyond descend to earth and the souls of mortals rise to heaven. This cosmic axle holds the world in balance and at the same time is its center."

When we use such ancient imagery, we are tapping into the vast shamanic knowledge that is our heritage from the earliest human tribes. I learned most of what I know about shamanism from Michael Harner, an anthropologist who has devoted a lifetime to the study of what he calls "classic core shamanism," shamanic techniques that are common to culture the world over and can be used by modern-day people to help themselves, others, and the planet as a whole. Many of his ideas are outlined in his book *The Way of the Shaman,* but the best way to learn these techniques is by taking his workshops, offered through the Foundation for Shamanic Studies.

Throughout human history, poets, priests, and visionaries have used a variety of methods for entering the inner world. The guided visualization technique we use is only one. A project of the Foundation for Shamanic Studies called Mapping of Nonordinary Reality, or MONOR, is based on the use of ancient techniques. Check the Resources section at the end of the book to explore other techniques.

When we begin these inner explorations, we learn about various resources we have stored within. I have a place near the trunk of my own tree where I go when I am very tired and need deep rest. In this place I feel perfectly safe and secure. My body evaporates, mingling with the atmosphere inside the tree, and only my eyes are left hanging there in the air, to mark where my body had been. When I whisk back to the original form of my body, I feel well rested and alert.

You may have discovered other areas inside yourself, places where memories and special skills are held in reserve until they are needed. We have now developed an effective way of moving about inside our tree and accessing what's in there. This technique is very useful for locating specific story material. Your voyages in your tree need not always have the purpose of collecting material for stories, though. If your children don't wish to speak about their voyages in the tree, that is their prerogative. Parents must allow their children the privacy to explore their inner worlds.

It may be that the very first stories were told in exactly this way, by shamans who made these voyages to the imagination and returned to tell their community what they had seen.

GUARDIAN ANIMALS

Many people meet a guardian or ally inside their tree. The guardian often takes the form of an animal. We all have symbolic animal companions in our lives: children have their teddy bears, and many adults have cars named after wild animals. In the following voyage we will go into our tree with the purpose of meeting an animal guide who can aid us in our explorations.

TIME: 20 minutes

GOAL: To make contact with a guardian animal in our tree.

PREPARATION: Prepare the room. Have blindfolds and paper and drawing materials on hand.

INSTRUCTIONS:

- "Let's lie quietly, with blindfolds on, enjoying the silence of the room." (Pause)
- "Go into your imagination now, into the field with your tree in its center."
- "Put your hands on the bark of your tree, embracing it in whatever way you like. If you wish, you may speak to the tree." (Pause)

VOYAGE 15

Locating a Guardian Animal

- "Go into your tree now, by way of the same entrance you used in the last voyage. Wait patiently at the entrance and ask your tree to send you a guardian who will guide you safely through your inner world. Look for an animal appearing before you. Listen to the tree: it may send you on a search for the animal. Follow your intuition to find your way. When you locate your animal guide, make eye contact with it. Speak to it with words or gestures or thoughts. Play with your animal and frisk about. Allow the animal to show you its special skills and talents. Do not concern yourself with learning anything now. Abandon yourself to the pleasure of frisking and playing with your animal." (5-minute pause)
- "Don't worry if you did not encounter an animal on this voyage. Simply make the voyage again later with the same intention."
- "Before you leave your animal guide, take a few moments to express any thoughts that you may have. Arrange a meeting place for yourselves for the next voyage. Perhaps your animal guide will teach you a song, a call, or some other device to help you to reestablish contact when you enter the tree the next time." (Pause)
- "Respectfully leave your animal now, exit the tree, and come back into your body, with your hands on the tree's bark."
- "Glance around your field. Take a last look at your tree. If there is something you wish to convey to the tree, do it now, using whatever manner of communication you and your tree have developed." (Pause)
- "Come out of imagination now, back into the room. Keep your eyes closed, rub your hands together, rub your face, and, when you are ready, open your eyes."
- "Make any additions to the map of your tree that you wish, using your drawing materials."
- "Your connection to your guardian animal is a very personal thing. Do not feel compelled to tell about your travels in the tree. If you do wish to share the details of your voyage with your family, though, you may do that now."
- "The voyage is now complete."

FEEDBACK: "I met a dog. I made eye contact with him, and he took me on an enjoyable run through his area, silently showing me many things," one boy said.

"I dove underwater down by the roots of the tree and swam with a fish," another boy remarked.

"I held on to a swan's back and circled up to the branches. I have always wanted to fly, and now I am able to," a girl said.

FOLLOW-UP TO VOYAGE 15: Meeting with a guardian animal is one of the most common shamanic experiences. Mircea Eliade, in his classic book *Shamanism*, writes: "The majority of these familiar and helping spirits have animal forms. Thus, among the Siberians and the people of the Altai Mountains, they can appear in the form of bears, wolves, stags, hares, all kinds of birds (especially the goose, eagle, owl, crow, etc.), and as great worms, but also as phantoms, wood spirits, earth spirits, hearth spirits, and so forth. Their forms, names, and numbers differ from region to region."

In his popular books about his encounters with the Yaqui Indian shaman don Juan, the anthropologist Carlos Castaneda also describes his encounters with a wide range of guardian animals, and how they lead him to new ways of perceiving the world.

For storytellers, the animal guide can be a great help in navigating the inner world. If an animal chases you or threatens you in the inner world, confront it and speak to it. If it appears in your tree, it is a potential ally. The animal that guides you through the tree is like a librarian walking you through the stacks. Even though the librarian may not have read every book in the library, he or she can still tell you where to find the information you need.

If at any time you become lost or confused in your tree, you can call for your guardian animal, and it will take you back to the place from which you can easily exit the tree.

TIME: 20 minutes

GOAL: To reestablish contact with our inner storyteller, the one in our inner world who tells stories truly and from the heart.

PREPARATION: Prepare the room. Have blindfolds and tree maps on hand.

VOYAGE 16

Awakening the Hidden Storyteller

INSTRUCTIONS:

- "Let's lie quietly, enjoying the silence."
- "Go into the imagination now, into your field, and put your hands on the bark of your tree."
- "Make contact with your guardian animal as you previously arranged. Exchange whatever greetings you like."
- "You and your guardian animal will be traveling through the tree now to locate the home of your inner storyteller. Your animal guide will be a help in locating this area. Respectfully explain to your guardian animal that you wish to locate the residence of your inner storyteller. Ask to have word sent ahead, by whatever means your animal guide has available, to alert your storyteller to your approach."
- "Set out now with your guardian animal to locate the home of your inner teller. If you encounter challenging forces on the way, trust your animal guide to help you through them. Once you have reached the home of your teller, stop, and wait there with your guardian animal before you actually make contact with your teller." (Pause)
- "Observe your teller's home carefully. If you plan to use the resources the inner teller can offer you, you will be returning here frequently. This is an important meeting for both of you. Your inner teller may have been silent, sleeping, or simply hiding until now. The inner teller has been yearning to make contact with you. Your work in this book has been beneficial for your teller, healing any wounds the teller may have suffered as a result of being ignored or silenced. All of the voyages you have made so far have been leading up to the moment of this meeting."
- "Approach with your animal guide the entrance of your teller's home. It may be a gate, a doorway, a rock passage, or a cluster of trees. Step inside the home of your storyteller now and greet whoever waits for you in whatever way you like. Look deeply into the eyes of your teller. This is the face you wore before the world was made. Take several moments now to reestablish contact with your inner storyteller." (5-minute pause)
- "Just as you did with your guardian animal, arrange to meet your teller again. Ask for instructions for signaling your return. Respectfully leave your teller in whatever

way seems right to you. Leave the home of your teller and ask your guardian animal to return you back to the entrance of your tree."

- "Respectfully leave your animal guide."
- "Come out of your tree with your hands on its bark. Address your tree if you wish."
- "Come out of imagination and back into your body in this room. Keep your eyes closed, rub your hands together, rub your face, and, whenever you are ready, open your eyes and come back into the room."

FEEDBACK: "When I looked into my teller's face, I saw that it was my face. I had been expecting some wise old man or some wise old woman, but I was surprised to find that it had been me all along," one woman said.

"My teller said that she had been waiting for me a long time and that I could come back to her as often as I wanted. She had no animosity toward me for ignoring her for so long," another woman reported.

A mother said, "My inner teller said, 'Don't worry; I'll help you with the stories.' Then she gave me a musical instrument—a harp—and showed me how to play it. That was strange because I never had any musical talent. I began to see that there is an intimate connection between appreciating music and appreciating stories."

FOLLOW-UP TO VOYAGE 16: The inner teacher is another ancient idea. In her book *Encounters with the Soul: Active Imagination,* Barbara Hannah describes a technique developed by Carl Jung for making contact with an inner teacher or guide. It involves entering the inner world and conversing with whatever inner teachers show themselves there. Hannah points out that the origins of this technique date back over four thousand years, to an account given in the *Egyptian Book of the Dead,* in which a world-weary man who wishes to die speaks to his soul and is surprised when it disagrees with him and instructs him to "follow the beautiful day and forget your sorrow."

The inner teller can be a great resource to you, whether you voyage to the teller's home to get specific instruction or simply call on the teller's guidance as you tell stories in the waking state. My own inner teller has supplied me with a workroom in which I can work on stories undisturbed, knowing that he is nearby if I need help with anything. Your inner teller will intuitively know what you need to learn and can be a great aid in developing your storytelling skills.

A LAST STORY

Now that you have an inner teller, you will have no further need for me. You have tools with which to voyage into the imagination and move about in time and inner space. I hope this quest into the imagination has been rewarding for you and your family. Many others have gone before us in this quest to explore the world of the storyteller. If we do our jobs well, many others will come after us.

Let's end this book, as we began it, with a story.

Long before our ancestors came to North America from other parts of the world, people had already been living here for thousands of years. Here is a story that comes to us from the Seneca Indian people, who lived in what is now upstate New York. I first heard this story through the Wampanoag storyteller Medicine Story. Medicine Story has recorded an excellent version of this legend on his audio tape *Tales of the Eastern Woodlands*. You can read another version of the story in Susan Feldman's *The Story Stone*. It tells of a time at the dawn of human history, when the very first story was told.

The Story Stone

Long ago, there lived a small boy among the Seneca people. He lived in a village at the edge of a great forest with his mother and father and his younger sister. And life was good for them. The men hunted for animals in the forest and hunted for fish in the streams. The women gathered healing herbs and grew corn, beans, and squash. The land provided everything they needed. But they weren't quite human yet. Because, you see, they didn't have any stories.

Long winter nights they would sit up by the fire, staring into the flames, and after they had said everything they wanted to say, there was nothing else to speak about, so they simply rolled over and went to sleep. You can imagine how boring that was.

Then one day, in the spring, the boy was out hunting birds

with his bow and arrow. He was getting to be a pretty good shot, and whenever he brought home a few birds at the end of the day, his parents praised him, and he felt good for being able to help out.

Then one day, while he was out hunting birds, he had a strange experience. He had shot a few birds and had come into a clearing in the forest. In the center of the clearing sat a large, rounded boulder. The boy sat down on the boulder to rest, laying his birds on top of the stone.

As the boy was sitting there, a voice right near him said, "Would you like to hear a story?"

The boy sprang up and looked around. He expected to see a man nearby. For it was a man's voice that had spoken, the voice of a very old man, full of gravel and wind. But there was no man near.

Then the voice said again, "Would you like to hear a story?"

The boy glanced around. Still he couldn't see anyone.

The voice said again, "Would you like me to tell you a story?"

It was then that the boy realized the voice was coming from the stone. He ran a few steps away, leaving his birds on top of the boulder.

"Leave me these birds and I will tell you a story," the voice of the stone offered.

The boy looked into the gray surface of the stone and thought he could make out the features of an old man.

"Who are you?" the boy asked, frightened. "And what are these things you're going to tell me? What are stories?"

"They are things that happened long ago. I am a Story Stone. I have been here for a long time, and I remember everything I have seen. Now that the humans are going to live here, it is time to pass a little of what we have learned along to them."

The boy was torn at first; part of him wanted to run, leaving his birds behind. But another part of him was curious. And there was something about the voice of the stone, something deep and rumbling, that fascinated him.

"You may have the birds," the boy said at last. "Now tell me one of these stories."

The stone began, "Long ago, in the far-off times, when the world was first made . . . ," and went on to tell how the world had been created and how the land had been formed and how the stars were set in the sky—all things the boy had wondered about. He had not known who to ask about these things, though.

The boy sat down in the meadow by the stone and listened the whole day, wide-eyed and open-mouthed.

The boy would have sat there all day and all night too, listening to those stories, which answered questions he hadn't even thought about. But at last, as the sun was dipping down, that stone said, "That is enough for now. You come back tomorrow and I'll tell you some more stories."

The boy left the birds on the rock and hurried home in the twilight. When his mother saw that he had been gone all day and hadn't brought back any birds, she said, "What were you doing out there?"

The boy answered as boys usually answer that question: "Oh, nothing."

That night, the mother called her daughter aside and said, "Listen, your brother is doing something out in the woods all day. I want you to follow him tomorrow and find out what he does out there."

"All right, Mother," the girl said.

The next day, the boy set out for the woods, eager to hear more stories. His sister followed him, being careful to keep back in the trees so he would not know she was there. She brought along her berry-picking basket so that she would have an excuse for being in the woods. She picked a few berries and dropped them in the basket just for show.

The girl watched as the boy shot two birds, then took them to a rounded boulder in the center of a clearing. She watched as her brother did a strange thing: he carefully laid the birds on top of the rock, then he sat down on the grass nearby and stayed sitting there for a long time. His sister wondered: What was he doing? Was this some special way of hunting? Was he setting a trap for some animal?

Peering through the bushes, she strained to see his face and noticed that he was listening very hard to something.

Carefully she slipped forward and then she heard it too—it was the voice of an old man, speaking in a way that she had never heard before. But she couldn't see anyone in the clearing except her brother. The girl was curious, and, since she was a straightforward kind of person, she walked right up to her brother and asked, "Who is that talking?" As soon as she spoke, the voice fell silent.

The boy spun around.

"Who is doing that talking?" she asked again.

The boy knew it was no use trying to fool his sister. "It's the Story Stone," he said. "Give it some berries and it will tell you a story."

"A story?" the girl asked. "What's a story?"

"Give it your berries and you'll find out," the boy said.

The girl was curious, so she scooped up a handful of berries from her basket and carefully placed them on top of the rock. Then she sat in the grass beside her brother.

"Welcome, sister," the stone said. "I was just telling your brother the story of how the deer got its antlers." And the Story Stone went on and told that story and another and another, told stories through the whole morning and afternoon, as the two children sat spellbound in the sunlit meadow.

At last the sun was dipping down, and the Story Stone said, "It's enough for one day. Come back tomorrow, and I'll tell you more."

The children walked home silently, thinking of the stories they had heard.

When their mother saw them coming back from the woods with only a few berries and maybe one bird to show for their day's work, she called the sister aside. "What was he doing out there?" the mother asked.

The girl just smiled. "Oh, nothing," she said.

That night, when the children went to sleep, they had wondrous dreams and began to see the things they had heard in the stories, dancing and singing. Their mother saw them smiling in their sleep. When her husband came in from hunting that night, she spoke to him quietly: "Our children are doing something out in the woods," she said. "I don't think it's bad, but it's something. Will you follow them tomorrow and find out what it is?" The husband agreed.

The next morning the boy and girl set out for the woods early, eager to hear more stories. Their father set out too, following them, taking along his fishing line so he would have an excuse to be in the woods. The boy shot a few birds, the girl picked some berries, and the man, just to look busy, caught a few fish.

The boy and girl came to the clearing where the Story Stone sat in the morning sun and carefully placed their gifts of food on the stone. The girl remarked that the food they placed the day before was gone.

"That's the way it is," the boy explained. "I think the stone sends his messengers the squirrels and the ants to carry the food away for him."

When the children had seated themselves, they heard the deep, comforting voice of the stone speaking, saying to them, "Welcome, children. Today I will tell you the story of how the first humans came to earth and how they learned to live here. . . ." And the stone began to speak.

Meanwhile, the father had been watching his children from the edge of the clearing. He saw his children sitting very still. And when he crept closer, he heard the voice, but he couldn't figure out where it was coming from. When he saw that his children were not in danger, he decided to wait patiently and see if he could figure it out. At last he understood that the children were listening to a voice coming from the stone. He was overcome with wonder.

The man stood up and walked into the clearing. As soon as he approached, the stone stopped speaking.

"What is this you have discovered?" the father asked.

The children laughed. "It's a Story Stone, Father. Give it one of your fish and it will tell you a story."

The man wrinkled his brow. "A story? What's that?"

"Give it your fish," the sister said, "and you'll find out!"

The man did as his daughter had told him, then sat down on the grass between his children.

The Story Stone spoke, its deep voice filling the meadow. "Welcome. It's a lucky man who comes to this place with his children. I was just telling them the story of how Rabbit taught the humans to make fire." And the Story Stone told tales the rest of the day as the father and his children sat, wide-eyed, listening together.

As the sun was dipping down, the stone said, "It is enough. Come back tomorrow, and I'll tell you more."

The children and their father rose and walked quietly back to the village. "We must share this great thing with your mother," the man said. And the children agreed.

That night after the children were asleep, the mother said, "Did you find out? What were they doing out there?"

The man smiled. "Yes, I found out and you were right. It isn't something bad, but it is something. They found a stone that tells stories."

The woman shook her head. "I don't understand. What's this thing you call a story?"

The man grinned. "Come with us tomorrow and you'll find out."

The next morning the whole family set out for the meadow, each bringing a small gift for the stone. The boy brought a bird, the girl brought some berries, the father brought a fish, and the mother, still unsure of what she was expected to do, brought along some corn she had grown.

When they arrived at the Story Stone, they placed their gifts on top of the rock and sat in the meadow. As the sun came up, the stone began to speak.

"Welcome. You are the first family in all creation to sit together and hear stories. It is a happy day for me. I will now tell you stories about how the humans came to know the animals and the plants. . . ." And the stone told stories all that day, as the family sat in the meadow, listening and dreaming along with the stone.

The boy thought that it was the best of all the days of storytelling he had heard. It delighted him to see his mother and father smiling and to see his sister's rapt attention when the Story Stone spoke.

At last, the sun dipped down and the forest began to darken. The stone finished its last story. Then the stone spoke to the family, saying, "This is a great day. But it is also a sad day for me. I have waited a long, long time to tell you these stories, and I have enjoyed telling them to you very much. But now my stories are ended, and I won't speak anymore."

The boy felt a stab of pain go through his heart.

"But that can't be!" he said. "Now that we have come to enjoy these stories, we don't want to be without them."

"You won't be without them," the stone answered, "because now *you* are the storytellers, and it will be your task to tell the stories to others, just as I have to you. Some of the people who will hear your stories will remember every part, and the stories will appear in their dreams, just as they have in yours. They will be the storytellers, and you should treat them well. Always give them a gift when they tell a story, just as you have done for me. Some of the people will only remember parts of the stories, and some of the people will forget the stories altogether. I think this is just how it will be. But if you keep the storytelling alive, you will never lose the stories I have told you.

"Farewell. I will remember these four days we have spent

together for thousands and thousands of years." Then the stone was silent.

The family walked home together in the twilight. When they got home, they built a huge fire and invited everyone in the village to come and sit with them at night. They told the other families about their adventure and their neighbors nodded their heads.

One old woman rose and said, "What you have told us is very interesting. But there is one thing I don't understand. What is this thing the stone gave you? This thing called a story?"

The boy laughed. "Give me a bit of that delicious corn bread you make, and I will show you!"

The woman gladly handed over a piece of the bread. The boy stood before the assembled village and began to speak, letting the images the stone had placed in his mind speak through him. He told the very first story the stone had told him on the first day they had met, about how the world had come to be. The people sat, listening and smiling and dreaming, as if they were one person. Then the boy went on and told the other stories he had learned. Late that night, the people carried their sleeping children home and as they fell into sleep, the village was filled with dreams.

In the nights that followed, each person in the boy's family took a turn, telling the stories the stone had given him or her. And it was just as the stone had said: Some people remembered the stories very well, and they told the stories to others. And some people forgot the stories. That, too, was just as the stone had said it would be.

Today, many of the old stories have been forgotten. That is true. But nothing is really lost. Some people say that the time has come for the stones to speak to us again, to tell us their stories, if we will only listen.

So let us open our ears and our hearts and hear what the stones are saying to us, calling us to remember, calling us back to the very first day when the very first stories were told.

The information listed here will help answer the question "Where do I go from here?"

As I have mentioned throughout the book, today's storytelling enthusiasts have a multitude of resources available to them. While I do not claim that this is a complete listing, it will show you a sampling of what is available.

The section is divided into two parts: listings and bibliography. In the listings section, you will find information on storytelling organizations, publications, and educational opportunities, as well as a nationwide calendar of major storytelling events. This information is reprinted with permission from the 1990 *National Directory of Storytelling,* published by the National Association for the Preservation and Perpetuation of Storytelling.

In the bibliography, I have listed books, tapes, and other resources mentioned in the book, as well as a sampling of other books that relate directly to the topics we explored in our voyages. Check your local library for these titles. If you don't find them there, you may be inspired to start assembling your own storytelling library at home.

A Guide to Story-telling Resources

Listings

Founded in 1975, the National Association for the Preservation and Perpetuation of Storytelling, or NAPPS, has spearheaded the storytelling renaissance in this country, and still remains the best single source for storytelling information and programming. If you want to find out what's happening in the storytelling network, I'd strongly advise you to join.

As I mentioned in the introduction, my own path in life was dramatically altered when I attended my first National Storytelling Festival in 1979. Since then, NAPPS has grown phenomenally. It continues to host the National Storytelling Festival each October, as well as a National Congress on Storytelling and an ongoing National Storytelling Institute.

You need not even leave your hometown to enjoy the benefits of joining NAPPS. Your membership dues bring you the quarterly *Storytelling Magazine* and *The Yarnspinner,* a storytelling newsletter with information about events in your area. NAPPS also publishes a *Catalog of Storytelling Resources* and a *National Directory of Storytelling.*

To receive information about joining NAPPS, write: NAPPS, P.O. Box 309, Jonesborough, TN 37659, or call (800) 525-4514.

Check the following information for storytelling happenings in your area.

ORGANIZATIONS AND CENTERS

Arizona

East Valley Teller of Tales. Dorothy Daniels Anderson, 4311 East Clarendon, Phoenix, AZ 85018. (602) 957-0462.

California

Community Storytellers. Kathleen Zundell, 19573 Cave Way, Topanga, CA 90290. (213) 455-2567.

The Desert Storytellers. Peggy Prentice, 1962 Baristo Rd., Palm Springs, CA 92262. (619) 322-4732.

Humboldt Storytellers. Olga Loya, P.O. Box 6766, Eureka, CA 95501. (707) 442-4228.

Katz Pajamas. Michael Katz, P.O. Box 91316, Santa Barbara, CA 93190. (805) 963-1385.

New Dimensions Radio. Michael or Justine Toms, P.O. Box 410510, San Francisco, CA 94141. (415) 563-8899.

Santa Cruz Storytellers. Lee-Ellen, 1110 Morrissey Blvd., Santa Cruz, CA 95065. (408) 458-2603.

Sonoma County Story Swap. Sandra MacLees, 6695 Westside Rd., Healdsburg, CA 95448. (707) 433-8728.

Storytellers of San Diego. Jim Dieckmann, 3406 Elliott St., San Diego, CA 92106. (619) 223-3078.

York House. John Harrell, 148 York Ave., Kensington, CA 94708.

Colorado

Boulder Storytellers Guild. Ann Cress, 4768 McKinley Dr., Boulder, CO 80303. (303) 444-1790.

Union Colony Storytellers' Guild. Helen E. Hanselmann, 2482 50th Ave., Greeley, CO 80634. (303) 330-6353.

Connecticut

Connecticut Storytelling Center. Department of Education, Connecticut College, New London, CT 06320. (203) 447-7738. Or Nancy Firth, 483 Colonial Rd., Guilford, CT 06437. (203) 453-4841.

Florida

Dancing Earth Network. John Rogers, 115 E. Ave. C, Melbourne, FL 32901. (407) 725-1923.

Florida Storytellers' Guild. Mitchell O'Rear, P.O. Box 540234, Orlando, FL 32854. (407) 645-3913.

Storytellers of Brevard. Lady Gail or Duchess of Magpie, 445 Nelson Dr., Merritt Island, FL 32953. (407) 452-6772.

The Storytelling Center. Ralph Wallenhorst, 5247 81st St. N., #24, St. Petersburg, FL 33709. (813) 545-4323.

The Storytellers' League of Jacksonville, Florida. Jan Hendrick, 1410 River Bluff Rd., Jacksonville, FL 32211. (904) 743-5095.

Talebearers, Jewish Storytellers Guild. Rabbi Rami M. Shapiro, P.O. Box 160081, Miami, FL 33116. (305) 235-1419.

Tallahassee Storytelling Guild. Shelley Harshbarger, 1936 Greenwood Dr., Tallahassee, FL 32303. (904) 386-4410.

Tamiami Tale Tellers Guild. Bert MacCarry, 498 Birdsong Pl., Sanibel, FL 33957. (813) 472-1781.

Georgia

Hunt School Storytellers (K-6). Jeannie Webb-Hodges, 990 Shurling Dr., Macon, GA 31211. (912) 742-7870.

Southern Order of Storytellers. Fiona Page, 1270 Woodstream Dr., Lawrenceville, GA 30244. (404) 381-7888.

Hawaii

Storytelling Association of Hawaii. Jeff Gere, 67313 Kiapoko Pl., Waialua, HI 96791. (808) 522-7029.

Illinois

North Shore Storytelling Guild. Kathleen Visovatti, 2127 Bennett Ave., Evanston, IL 60201. (708) 328-5228.

Riverbend Storytelling Guild. Catherine Cooney, 1005 25th Ave. Ct., Moline, IL 61265 (309) 797-3257.

Sangamon Storytelling Guild. Dr. David Hilligoss, Sangamon State University, Springfield, IL 62708. (217) 786-6789.

Indiana

The Northern Indiana Storytelling Guild. Bob or Kathie Myers, 1225 E. Third St., Mishawaka, IN 46544. (219) 255-5058.

Stories, Inc. Bob Sander, P.O. Box 20743, Indianapolis, IN 46220. (317) 255-7628.

Iowa

RiverTellers. Duffy De France, RR 2 Lot 219, Muscatine, IA 52761. (319) 263-1736.

Iowa Storytelling Guild. Contact Gail Froyen, 1611 W. 18th St., Cedar Falls, IA 50613. (319) 266-8700.

Storytellers Roundtable. Iowa Library Association, 823 Insurance Exchange Building, Des Moine, IA 50309. (515) 243-2172.

Fireside Consortium of Storytellers. Deanne Wortman, Iowa City Public Library, 123 S. Linn St., Iowa City, IA 52240.

Kansas

J.T. Productions (Gospel Storytellers). Joyce Todd, P.O. Box 12021, Kansas City, KS 66112. (913) 334-6190.

Kentucky

Bluegrass Storyweavers. Tandra J. White-Jennings, 1384 Tanforan Dr., Lexington, KY 40517. (606) 273-2376.

Louisiana

The Good Fairies of Hullen Ridge, Inc. Jane S. Kreisman, 509 Williams Blvd., Kenner, LA 70062. (504) 464-1410.

StoryFest. Rose Anne St. Romain, Lafayette Public Library, P.O. Box 3427, Lafayette, LA 70502. (318) 261-5775.

Maryland

Frederick Area Talespinners. Kathleen Rudesill, 105 Lombardy Dr., Middletown, MD 21769. (301) 293-6816.

Phoenix, Celebrating the Arts in Religion and Community. Jorja Davis, Drawer C, Odenton, MD 21113. (301) 674-5323.

Massachusetts

Cape and Islands Storytellers Collaborative. Julie Meltzer, 46 Shallow Pond Ln., E. Falmouth, MA 02536. (508) 457-1224.

Jewish Storytelling Coalition. Hanna Bandes, 19 Englewood Ave., Brookline, MA 02146. (617) 738-0480.

League for the Advancement of New England Storytelling (LANES). Elisa Pearmain, P.O. Box 1483, Arlington, MA 02174. (617) 396-5363.

Oak and Stone Storytellers. Katie Green and Cheryl Savageal, P.O. Box 1212, Worcester, MA 01613. (508) 464-5146.

Michigan

Detroit Story League. Jean Gordon, 18858 Jamestown Ci., Northville, MI 48167. (313) 348-9177.

Community Storytellers. Ralph C. Morrison, P.O. Box 521, Oshtemo, MI 49077. (616) 372-4368.

Minnesota

Longfellow Educators Story League. Larry Johnson, 2615 S. 6th St., Minneapolis, MN 55454. (612) 333-0970.

OGP (Old Gardening Party). Larry Johnson, Box 9907, Minneapolis, MN 55458. (612) 333-0970.

Salt of the Earth: A Biblical Storytelling Circle. Sarah Meybaum, 3522 Harriet Ave. S., #205, Minneapolis, MN 55408. (612) 825-3965.

Senior Saga Spinners. Leona Classen, Box 42, Alberta, MN 56207. (612) 324-2634.

Missouri

Creative Play. Marlene Katz, 8700 Belleview, Kansas City, MO 64114. (816) 361-0890.

Gateway Storytellers. Roger Rose, 527 Greeley Ave., Webster Groves, MO 63119. (314) 961-6251.

Midwest Storytelling Theatre. Susan Sylvia Scott, 9100 Cherry, Kansas City, MO 64131. (816) 444-5537.

MO-TELL (Missouri Storytelling). Perrin Stifel, 636 Elmwood, St. Louis, MO 63119. (314) 961-3948.

Tale-A-Visions. Jim "Two Crows" Wallen, 608 E. Kansas, Independence, MO 64050. (816) 254-6510.

Unity Storytelling Guild. Janet Bowser Manning, The Arches, Unity Village, MO 64065. (816) 525-1776.

New Jersey

Garden State Storytellers' League. Carol Satz, 2100 Lawrenceville Rd., Lawrenceville, NJ 08648. (609) 896-2746.

The New Jersey Storytellers Circle. Julie Della Torre, 47 Henry St., Glen Rock, NJ 07452.

New Jersey Storytelling Guild. Gerald Fierst, 222 Valley Rd., Montclair, NJ 07042. (201) 746-4608.

New Mexico

Library Storytellers. Kathy Costa, 1730 Llano St., Santa Fe, NM 87505. (605) 473-7263.

New York

Association for Library Service to Children: Storytelling Discussion Group. Mary Ann Gilpatrick or Rita Auerbach, 2 Shore Rd., E. Patchogue, NY 11772. (516) 475-3431.

Jewish Storytelling Center. Peninnah Schram, Director, 525 West End Ave., 8C, New York, NY 10024. (212) 787-0626.

New York City Storytelling Center. Billie Ballou, Director, 190 Haverstraw Rd., Suffern, NY 10901. (914) 357-0504.

Pearl in the Egg Storytelling Guild. Eileen Moeller, Box 780, Kellogg St., Clinton, NY 13323. (315) 853-2558.

Pickney Production. Malika Lee Whitney, 1925 Manhattanville Station, Harlem, NY 10027. (212) 969-0779.

The Rye Storytellers' Guild. Judy Greenfield/Neva Winter, The Rye Free Reading Room, 1061 Boston Post Rd., Rye, NY 10580. (914) 967-0480.

Southern Tier Storytellers. Paul Leone, 134 Lakeview Ave., Jamestown, NY 14701. (716) 664-2997.

Story Circle of the Capital District. Lois Foight Hodges, RD 1, Box 189, Esperance, NY 12066. (518) 875-6008 or (518) 382-3513.

Westchester Storytellers' Guild. Miriam Budin or Agnes Griesar, 174

Rosedale Ave., Hastings-on-Hudson, NY 10706. (914) 478-5584.

North Carolina

Carolinas Association for the Preservation and Perpetuation of Storytelling. Ron Robinson, 7745 Ridgeloch Pl., Charlotte, NC 28226. (704) 543-8883.

Piedmont Storytelling Festival. Steven Henegar, Visiting Artist, Guilford Technical Community College, P.O. Box 309, Jamestown, NC 27282. (919) 454-1126, ext. 2412.

Artsplosure, The Raleigh Arts Festival, Inc. Merle Smith Creech, P.O. Box 590, Raleigh, NC 27602. (919) 890-3196.

Ohio

Miami Valley Storytellers. (Dayton Area). Sharon Luster, P.O. Box 292791, Kettering, OH 45429. (513) 436-9583.

Ohio Order for the Preservation of Storytelling. Lilly Marge Kelly, P.O. Box 5015, Cincinnati, OH 45205. (513) 921-8337.

Oregon

Eugene Storyteller's Association. Yvonne Young, 1975 Olive, Eugene, OR 97405. (503) 344-4693.

Troupe of Tellers. Robert E. Rubinstein, Roosevelt Middle School, 640 E. 24th, Eugene, OR 97405.

Pennsylvania

Hola Kumba Ya Cultural Arts Organization. Imani Lumumba, P.O. Box 50173, Philadelphia, PA 19132. (215) 848-5118.

Patchwork: A Storytelling Guild. Barbara Baumgartner, 518 W. Clapier St., Philadelphia, PA 19144. (215) 849-8783.

Storytellers Unlimited. Michael P. Snyder, Peters Twp. Public Library, 610A E. McMurray Rd., McMurray, PA 15317. (412) 941-9430.

Tapestry of Tales South Central Pennsylvania Storytelling Guild. Marie Winger, 1280 Fawnwood Dr., Lancaster, PA 17601. (717) 898-0856.

Rhode Island

State-line Storytellers. Jeanne Donato, RR4, 82 Potter Hill Rd., Westerly, RI 02891. (401) 596-0886.

South Carolina

Charleston Back Porch Storytellers. Terrence Larimer, 732 Woodward Rd., Charleston, SC 29407. (803) 571-5936.

Tennessee

GRITS. Victoria Elliott, 5103 Elkins Ave., Nashville, TN 37209. (615) 259-6276 or Nancy Cain, 504 Chesterfield Ave., Nashville, TN 37212. (615) 385-2140.

Jackson Story League. Lottie Mann, 14 Fair Oaks Dr., Jackson, TN 38305. (901) 668-7936.

National Association for the Preservation and Perpetuation of Storytelling (NAPPS). P.O. Box 309, Jonesborough, TN 37659. (615) 753-2171.

The Tennessee Association for the Preservation and Perpetuation of Storytelling (TAPPS). Dr. Flora Joy, President, ETSU Box 21910A, Johnson City, TN 37614. (615) 929-4297—or—Bev Twillmann, 9337 Millstone Lane, Knoxville, TN 37922. (615) 694-9988.

Teller of Tales Story League. Mildred J. Sanders, 636 Marlboro Ave., Chattanooga, TN 37412. (615) 698-1916.

Texas

Houston Storytellers Guild. Sally Goodroe or Jim Ohmart, 1525 West Main #4, Houston, TX 77006. (713) 523-3289 or 674-2528.

National Story League. Elizabeth Raabe, 52 Stephen F. Austin Dr., Conroe, TX 77302. (804) 794-3336.

Tarrant Area Guild of Storytellers. Kristie Kirchoff, 1201 S. Main, Grapevine, TX 76148. (817) 656-0373.

Tejas Storytelling Association. Finley Stewart, 110 C. West Oak, Denton, TX 76201. (817) 565-1968.

Virginia

Fredericksburg Storytellers. Caroline S. Parr, Central Rappahannock Regional Library, 1201 Caroline St., Fredericksburg, VA 22401. (703) 372-1144.

KI Theatre (formerly Golden Key). Julie Portman, P.O. Box 203, Washington, VA 22747. (703) 987-3164.

Washington

Olympia Storytelling. Debe Edden, 319 N. Foote, Olympia, WA 98502. (206) 943-6772.

Schooltelling. Cathy Spagnoli, 5646 25th S.W., Seattle, WA 98106. (206) 937-8679.

Seattle Storytellers' Guild. Naomi Baltuck, P.O. Box 45532, Seattle, WA 98145-0532. (206) 621-8646.

Washington, D.C.

Voices in the Glen, Ltd. Margaret Chatham, 2631 Kirklyn St., Falls Church, VA 22043. (703) 698-5456.

Wisconsin

M.A.S.T. (Milwaukee Area Story Tellers Guild). S. Jean Andrew, 6023 W. Lincoln Ave., Milwaukee, WI 53219. (414) 327-5585.

Canada

T.A.L.E.S. (The Alberta League Encouraging Storytelling). Gail de Vos, 10523-100 Ave., Edmonton, Alberta, Canada, T5J 0A8. (403) 424-7764.

The Second Story Workshop. Mary-Eileen McClear, 89 Snyders Rd. W., Baden, Ontario N0B 1G0. (519) 634-8973.

The Storytellers School of Toronto. Carol Howe, 412A College St., Toronto, Ontario M5T 1T3. (416) 924-8625.

Stone Soup Stories of Winnipeg. Mary-Louise Quanbury, 35 Cordova St., Winnipeg, Manitoba R3N 0W7. (204) 489-6994.

Germany

Theaterdilldopp. Stefan Kuntz, Maria-Hilf-Strasse 9, D-5000 Koin 1, F.R. of Germany. Tele 02 21/32 87 58.

Ireland

Siamsa MacManus. Fiountan Gogarty, Donegal Craft Village, Donegal, Co. Donegal, Ireland. Tele (073) 22015.

Northern Ireland

The Yarnspinners. Liz Weir, Linen Hall Library, Belfast, Liz Weir, 38 Lismurn Park, Ahoghill, County Antrim, BT421JN, Northern Ireland, Tele (U.K.) 0266 871583.

Venezuela

TAPICNO: Taller Permanente de Investigación y Creación en Narración Oral. Daniel Mato, Magdamar (9-A) Au Ppal. de Santa Fe Sur, Caracas-1080, Venezuela. Tele 979-8448.

EVENTS

Alabama

Bayside Yarnspinners Festival • Mobile, Alabama • April • Connie Smith, (205) 471-1315.

Arizona

Storytelling Concert • Scottsdale Amphitheatre, Scottsdale Mall, Scottsdale, Arizona • April • Dorothy Daniels Anderson, 4311 E. Clarendon, Phoenix AZ 85018. (602) 957-0462.

California

By Word of Mouth • Pasadena, California • October–May • Kind Crone Productions, 582 Eldora Rd., Pasadena, CA 91104. (818) 797-6817.

Community Storytellers • Wildwood School, Santa Monica, CA • 2nd Thursday each month at 7 pm • Kathleen Zundell, 19573 Cave Way, Topanga, CA 90290.

Storytelling • Prescott Hotel, San Francisco, California • Ongoing • 545 Post St., San Francisco, CA 94102 (415) 563-0303.

Family Radio Storytelling Program • KCSB 91.9 FM (public radio), Santa Barbara, California • Michael Katz, P.O. Box 91316, Santa Barbara, CA 93190. (805) 963-1385.

Humboldt Storytellers at Casa de Que Pasa Restaurant • Arcata, California • February, April, June, September, and November • Olga Loya, P.O. Box 6766, Eureka, CA 95501. (707) 442-4228.

Mariposa County Storytelling Festival • Mariposa County Fairgrounds, Mariposa, California • March • Workshops and performances. College credit available • Linda Johnson, P.O. Box 425, Mariposa, CA 95338. (209) 966-2456.

Pacific Southwest Regional Festival • Berkeley, California • August • Lewis Mahlmann, 707 East 24th St., Oakland, CA 94606.

Sierra Storytelling Festival • Schoolhouse Cultural Center, Nevada City, California • July • Steve Sanfield, 17894 Tyler-Foote Rd., Nevada City, CA 95959. (916) 265–2826.

Southern California Storyswapping Festival • University of San Diego • May • Jim Dieckmann, 3406 Elliott St., San Diego, CA 92106. (619) 223-3078.

Storytelling Potlucks • Santa Cruz, California • First Sunday of each month • Lee-Ellen, 1110 Morrissey Blvd., Santa Cruz, CA 95065. (408) 458-2603.

Summer Solstice Folk Music and Dance Festival • California State University, Northridge, California • June • Elaine Weismann, 4401 Trancas Pl., Tarzana, CA 91356. (818) 342-7664.

Winter Tales Series • Schoolhouse Cultural Center, Nevada City, California • November through February • 17894 Tyler-Foote Rd., Nevada City, CA 95959. (916) 265-2826.

Colorado

Rocky Mountain Storytelling Festival • Palmer Lake, Colorado • August • John Stansfield, Box 588, Monument, CO 80132. (719) 481-3202.

Connecticut

Connecticut Storytelling Festival • Connecticut Storytelling Center, Connecticut College, New London, Connecticut • April • Barbara Reed, Old Quarry, Guilford, CT 06437. (203) 447-7738 or (203) 453-3630.

Connecticut Student Storytelling Festival • Wesleyan University, Middletown, Connecticut • May • Rosalind Hinman, 1 Smith Neck Rd., Old Lyme, CT 06371. (203) 434-9012.

Tales Told Under an Apple Tree: Storyfests • Bethel, Connecticut • 2nd and 3rd weekends in September and 2nd and 3rd weekends in October • Mary Patterson, Blue Jay Orchards, Plumtrees Rd., Bethel, CT 06801. (203) 748-0119 or (203) 744-4307.

Florida

Cocoa, Florida Storyfest '90 • Merritt Island, Florida • April • Lady Gail or Duchess of Magpie, 445 Nelson Dr., Merritt Island, FL 32953. (407) 452-6772.

End of Summer Celebration (Tales of Suspence and the Unexplainable Plus) • October • Lady Gail or Duchess of Magpie, 445 Nelson Dr., Merritt Island, FL 32953. (407) 452-6772.

Florida Storytelling Camp • Leesburg, Florida • March • Mitchell O'Rear, P.O. Box 540234, Orlando, FL 32854 (407) 645-3913.

Monthly Story Swap Sessions • Canterbury School, Fort Myers, Florida • Third Wednesday of each month • Bert MacCarry, 498 Birdsong Pl., Sanibel, FL 33957. (813) 472-1781.

Super-Duper Summer Storytelling Festival • Miami, Florida • June • Main Library, 101 W. Flagler St., Miami, FL 33130.

Georgia

Atlanta Storytelling Festival • Atlanta Historical Society, Atlanta, Georgia • April • Fiona Page, 1270 Woodstream Dr., Lawrenceville, GA 30244. (404) 381-7888.

Cherry Blossom Storytelling Concert • Theatre Macon, Macon, Georgia • March • Jeannie Webb-Hodges, 990 Shurling Dr., Macon, GA 31211. (912) 742-7870 or (912) 474-9218.

Olde Christmas Storytelling Festival • Callonwolde Fine Arts Center, Atlanta, Georgia • January • Fiona Page, 1270 Woodstream Dr., Lawrenceville, GA 30244. (404) 381-7888.

Southeast Regional Festival of Puppeteers of America • Helen, Georgia • August • Pat Minnaugh, 2731 Taft St., Apt. C-303, Hollywood, FL 33020.

Hawaii

The Gathering with Lucille Brenneman • April • Jeff Gere, 67313 Kiapoko Pl., Waialua, HI 96791. (808) 522-7029 (weekdays).

Talking Island Festival • McCoy Pavillion, Ala Moana Park, Honolulu, Hawaii • October • Jeff Gere, 67313 Kiapoko Pl., Waialua, HI 96791. (808) 522-7029.

Illinois

Blossom Time Storytelling Festival • Lincoln Memorial Garden by Lake Springfield, Springfield, Illinois • April • Dr. David Hilligoss, Sangamon State University, Springfield, IL 62708. (217) 786-6789.

Ghost Stories at Clayville • Clayville Historic Site, Springfield, Illinois • Sunday evening before Halloween • Dr. David Hilligoss, Sangamon State University, Springfield, IL 62708. (217) 786-6789.

Ghost Stories by Riverbend Storytelling Guild • Riverside Park, Moline, Illinois • October • Catherine Cooney, 1005 25th Ave. Court, Moline, IL 61265. (309) 797-3257.

Great Lakes Regional Festival of Puppeteers of America • Schaumburg, Illinois • July • Fred Putz, 2580 Oak St., Highland Park, IL 60035.

Illinois Storytelling Festival • Village Park Off Main Street, Spring Grove, Illinois • July • Jim May, P.O. Box 1012, Woodstock, IL 60098. (815) 648-2039.

Storytelling Discussion Group—Association for Library Service to Children • Meets twice a year at American Library Association annual and midwinter conferences • June in Chicago, Illinois • January in Chicago, Illinois • Mary Ann Gilpatrick or Rita Auerbach, 2 Shore Rd., E. Patchogue, NY 11772. (516) 475-3431.

Wild Onion Storytelling Celebration • Winnetka, Illinois • February • Kathleen Visovatti, 2127 Bennett Ave., Evanston, IL 60201. (708) 328-5228.

Indiana

Hoosier Storytelling Festival • Indianapolis, Indiana • August • Bob Sander, P.O. Box 20743, Indianapolis, IN 46220. (317) 255-7628.

Iowa

Bix Riverbend Storytelling Festival • Davenport, Iowa • July • Held in conjunction with the Bix Arts Festival • Catherine Cooney, 1005 25th Ave. Ct., Moline, IL 61265. (309) 757-3257.

Cedar River Storytelling Festival • Wartburg College • Third Tuesday in September • Englebrecht Library, Wartburg College, Waverly, IA 30677. (319) 352-1200 or Northeastern Iowa Regional Library System, 619 Mulberry St., Waterloo, IA 50703. (319) 233-1200.

ILA Storytellers Roundtable • Annual program at the Iowa Library Association convention • October of each year at various sites around Iowa • Duffy De France, RR2, Lot 219, Muscatine, IA 52761.

The Iowa Storytelling Festival • Clear Lake, Iowa • Last weekend in July • Clear Lake Public Library, 200 N. 4th St., Clear Lake, IA 50428. (515) 357-6133.

POPO's Puppet Festival • Iowa City Public Library • Saturday after Thanksgiving • Deanne Wortman or Debb Green, Iowa City Public Library, 123 S. Linn, Iowa City, IA 52240. (318) 356-5200.

Louisiana

Children's Book Week • Lafayette Public Library, Lafayette, Louisiana • November • Rose Anne St. Romain, Lafayette Public Library, P.O. Box 3427, Lafayette, LA 70502. (318) 261-5775.

The Fantasy College • Kenner, Louisiana • Saturday mornings • Jane S. Kreisman, 509 Williams Blvd., Kenner, LA 70062. (504) 464-1410.

Maine

Jackson and Friends • St. Saviour's Parish House, Bar Harbor, ME • "Weeknights Live!" • Tuesday through Thursday, July through September • Jackson Gillman, HCR 62 Box 36A, Mt. Desert, ME 04660. (207) 244-3838.

Maryland

Washington Storytelling Festival • Glen Echo Park, Glen Echo, Maryland • May • George Mason Law Center, Arlington, Virginia • May • Workshops and adult performances • Paul Van Gulick, P.O. Box 21256, Washington, DC 20009. (202) 462-0679.

Tapestry of Talent Student Storytelling Festival • Frostburg State University, Frostburg, Maryland • March • Dr. Gail Neary Herman, Rt. 2, Lodge Circle, Swanton, MD 21561. (301) 387-9199.

Massachusetts

Stories After Dark • Brookline, Massachusetts • October through May • Betty Lehrman or Sharon Kennedy, 99 Arlington St., Brighton, MA 02135. (617) 254-5035.

Sharing the Fire '90, Storytelling: Pathway to Discovery • Boston University • Annual March conference • Elisa Pearmain, P.O. Box 1483,

Arlington, MA 02174. (617) 396-5363.

Festival of Storytelling on Martha's Vineyard • Oak Bluffs, Massachusetts • June • Susan Klein, Box 214, Oak Bluffs, MA 02557. (508) 693-4140 or 693-0245.

Three Apples Storytelling Festival • Town of Harvard, Massachusetts • October • P.O. Box 994, Cambridge, MA 02238. (617) 628-5865.

Storytellers in Concert Storytelling Concert Series • Boston University, Cambridge, Massachusetts • September–June • Robert Smyth, P.O. Box 994, Cambridge, MA 02238. (617) 628-5865.

Michigan

Renaissance City Storyfest • General Lectures Building, Wayne State University, Detroit, Michigan • May • Dr. William Alfred Boyce, 585 Manoogian Hall, Wayne State University, Detroit, MI 48202. (313) 577-6296.

Scotts Mill Storytelling Festival • Scotts Mill, Scotts, Michigan • August • Ralph C. Morrison, P.O. Box 521, Oshtemo, MI 49077. (616) 372-4368.

Storytelling '90 • Henry Ford Community College, Dearborn, Michigan • October • Barbara Schutz, 2825 Kimberly, Ann Arbor, MI 48104. (313) 761-5118.

Minnesota

Big Woods Storytelling Festival • Nerstrand State Park • June • Marie Vogl Gery, 107 First St., Dundas, MN 55019. (507) 645-4644.

Storytelling for Adults • Seward Cafe, Minneapolis, Minnesota • Every Friday night, 8–10, all year long • Larry Johnson, Box 9907, Minneapolis, MN 55458. (612) 333-0970, or Maven Hinderlie (612) 825-9479.

Salt of the Earth: A Biblical Storytelling Circle • Beautiful Saviour Lutheran Church, New Hope, Minnesota • Third Sunday of each month • Sarah Meybaum, 3522 Harriet

Ave. So. #205, Minneapolis, MN 55408. (612) 825-3965.

Biblical Storytelling Workshop • Mt. Carmel Camp, Alexandria, Minnesota • August–September • Sonja Hinderlic, Mt. Carmel Ministries, P.O. Box 26, Minneapolis, MN 55458. (612) 521-3794.

Mississippi

Magnolia Storytelling Festival • Longwood Memorial Park, Natchez, Mississippi • September • Berry G. Bateman, 201 Dunbarton, Natchez, MS 39120. (601) 442-9407.

Missouri

Great Plains Regional Festival of Puppeteers of America • Kansas City, Missouri • July • Paul Mesner, 3615 Holmes, Kansas City, MO 64109.

MO-TELL Cuivre River State Park Storytelling Weekend • Troy, Missouri • October • Perrin Stifel, 636 Elmwood, St. Louis, MO 63119. (314) 961-3948.

MO-TELL Lake of the Ozarks State Park Storytelling Weekend • April • Perrin Stifel, 636 Elmwood, St. Louis, MO 63119. (314) 961-3948.

New Jersey

Pumpkin Patch Festival with Kathryn Farnsworth • Abma's Farm, New Jersey • October (Raindate, October 27) • Abma's Farm, 700 Lawlins Rd., Wyckoff, NJ 07481. (201) 891-0278.

Sixteenth Children's Literature and Storytelling Conference • Forcina Hall, Trenton State College, Trenton, New Jersey • October • Eileen Burke or Gwendolyn Jones, Forcina Hall #333, Trenton State College, Hillwood Lakes CN 4700, Trenton, NJ 08650-4700. (609) 771-2465.

New York

Big Apple Storytelling Festival • New York City • June • Several sites in different boroughs of New York City • Marcia Lane, 462 Amsterdam Ave., New York, NY 10024. (212) 799–1196.

Jewish Storytelling Center • 92nd Street YM-YWHA (Library), New York, NY • Third Thursday of each month, September through May • Annual Conference, August, in Columbus, Ohio • Peninnah Schram, 525 West End Ave., #8-C, New York, NY 10024. (212) 787-0626.

Long Island Summer Storytelling Festival • Heckscher Park, Huntington, and Sayville Junior High School, Sayville, New York • July • Heather Forest, Cartoon Opera, P.O. Box 354, Huntington, NY 11743. (516) 271-2511.

New York City Storytelling Center Riverside Tales Festival • Riverside Park, Manhattan • Sundays at 2 p.m. in July and August • Julian Rubenstein, 349 11th St., Brooklyn, NY 11215. (718) 832-0239.

New York City Storytelling Center Workshops • New York City • Second Wednesday of every month for workshops and third Wednesday of every month for story swaps • Julian Rubenstein, 349 11th St., Brooklyn, NY 11215. (718) 832-0239.

Pickney Productions Folktales for a Fools Day • Harlem School of the Arts, Harlem, New York • April • Malika Lee Whitney, 1925 Manhattanville Station, Harlem, NY 10027. (212) 969-0779.

Storyfest '90 • The Gathering Place, Norwich, New York • November • Jean Eastman, 11 W. Main St., Norwich, NY 13815. (607) 334-8909.

North Carolina

Artsplosure Autumn Jazz and Heritage Festival • Downtown Raleigh, North Carolina • September • The Raleigh Arts Festival, Inc., Merle Smith Creech, P.O. Box 590, Raleigh, NC 27602. (919) 890-3196.

Artsplosure Spring Arts Festival • Downtown Raleigh, North Carolina • April–May • The Raleigh Arts Festival, Inc., Merle Smith Creech, P.O. Box 590, Raleigh, NC 27602. (919) 890-3196.

Fall Storytelling Festival • Fletcher

Park, Raleigh, North Carolina •
September • Ron I. Jones, 4020
Carya Dr., Raleigh, NC 27610.
(919) 839-7133.

Piedmont Storytelling Festival •
Greensboro/High Point, North
Carolina • The Broach Theatre, The
High Point Theatre, GTCC Campus • April • Steven Henegar, Visiting Artist, Guilford Technical
Community College, P.O. Box 309,
Jamestown, NC 27282. (919) 454-
1126, ext. 2412.

Ohio

Create, International Conference •
John Carroll University, Cleveland,
Ohio • July • Jorja Davis, Drawer C,
Odenton, MD 21113. (301) 674-
5323.

Dayton Storytelling Festival • Carillon
Historical Park, Dayton, Ohio •
Sundays, May • Sharon Luster, P.O.
Box 292791, Kettering, OH 45429.
(513) 436-9583.

*Ohio State Storytelling Festival
(OOPS!)* • Chesterville, Ohio • May
• Lilly Marge Kelly, P.O. Box 5015,
Cincinnati, Ohio 45205. (513) 921-
8337.

Zanesville Storyfest • Ohio University–Zanesville Center and area
schools, Zanesville, Ohio • September • David Mitzel, OU–Zanesville
Campus, 1425 Newark Rd., Zanesville, OH 43701. (614) 453-0762.

Oklahoma

SunFest Storytelling Festival • Bartlesville, Oklahoma • June • Fran Stallings, 1406 Macklyn Ln., Bartlesville, OK 74006. (918) 333-7390.

Oregon

*Twentieth Anniversary of the Troupe
of Tellers* • Hult Center for the Performing Arts, Soreng Theatre, Eugene, Oregon • May • Robert E. Rubinstein, Roosevelt Middle School,
640 E. 24th, Eugene, OR 97405.
(503) 687-3228.

Pennsylvania

*Mid-Atlantic/Northeast 1990 Regional Festival of Puppeteers of
America* • Bryn Mawr, Pennsylvania • June • Robert Smythe, 13 W.
Biddle St., West Chester, PA 19380.

Mid-Atlantic Storytellers Gathering •
Millersville University, Millersville,
Pennsylvania • July • Marie Winger,
1280 Fawnwood Dr., Lancaster,
PA 17601. (717) 898-0856.

Rhode Island

Jonnycake Storytelling Festival • Village Green, Peace Dale, Rhode Island • September • 325 Columbia
St., Peace Dale, RI 02883. (401)
789-9301.

South Carolina

A(ugusta) Baker's Dozen • Columbia,
South Carolina • April • Richland
County Public Library, 1400 Sumter St., Columbia, SC 29201. (803)
799-9084.

Live Oak Storytelling Festival •
Charleston, South Carolina • October • Terrence Larimer, 732 Woodward Rd., Charleston, SC 29407.
(803) 571-5936.

Tennessee

Halloween Storyfest • East Tennessee
State University, Johnson City • October • Dr. Flora Joy, ETSU, Box
21910A, Johnson City, TN 37614.
(615) 929-4297.

TAPPS Annual Storytelling Festival •
Memphis, TN • June • Tennessee
Association for the Preservation
and Perpetuation of Storytelling
(TAPPS) • Dr. Flora Joy, ETSU, Box
21910A, Johnson City, TN 37614.
(615) 929-4297.

The National Storytelling Festival •
Jonesborough, Tennessee • October
• NAPPS, P.O. Box 309, Jonesborough, TN 37659. (615) 753-
2171.

The National Congress on Storytelling • Co-Sponsored by Northlands
Storytelling Network • June •
Minneapolis–St. Paul, Minnesota •
NAPPS, P.O. Box 309, Jonesborough, TN 37659. (615) 753-
2171.

Texas

Armand Bayou Tale Tellin' Festival • Armand Bayou Nature Center, Houston, Texas • First full weekend in May • Co-sponsored by the Houston Storytellers Guild and the Armand Bayou Nature Center • Sally Goodroe or Jim Ohmart, 1525 W. Main #4, Houston, TX 77006. (713) 523-3289 or (713) 674-2528.

Tellabration Texas! • Occurs throughout the state, at Denton, Dallas, Ft. Worth, Odessa, Houston, San Antonio, Austin, and Amarillo. • November • Finley Steward, 110 C. West Oak, Denton, TX 76201. (817) 565-1968.

Texas Storytelling Festival • Denton, Texas, Texas Women's University • March • Finley Stewart, 110 C. West Oak, Denton, TX 76201, (817) 565-1968.

Vermont

Vermont Storytelling Festival • Burlington, Vermont • November • Peter Burns, 205 King St., Burlington, VT 05401. (802) 658-3654.

Virginia

Busch Gardens Storytelling Festival • Busch Gardens, The Old Country, Williamsburg, Virginia • May • Busch Gardens Storytelling Festival, Group Sales Department, One Busch Gardens Blvd., Williamsburg, VA 23187-8785. (804) 253-3350.

Washington

At the Boiserie • Boiserie Coffee House, Seattle, Washington • First and third Fridays, monthly • Naomi Baltuck, P.O. Box 45532, Seattle, WA 98145-0532. (206) 621-8646.

Northwest Storytelling Festival • Seattle, Washington • February • Naomi Baltuck, P.O. Box 45532, Seattle, WA 98145-0532. (206) 621-8646.

Washington, D.C.

Elva Young Van Winkle Storytelling Festival • Washington, D.C. • November • Maria Salvadore, 901 G. St., N.W., Washington, D.C. 20001. (202) 727-1151.

Wisconsin

Halloween Ghost Story Telling Festival • Mt. Horeb, Wisconsin • Weekend before Halloween • Reid Miller, Box 178, Blue Mounds, WI 53517-0178. (608) 437-3388.

M.A.S.T. (Milwaukee Area Story Tellers Guild) • Mount Mary College, Milwaukee, Wisconsin • Storytelling every 3rd Friday • S. Jean-Andrew, 6023 W. Lincoln Ave., Milwaukee, WI 53219. (414) 327-5585.

Canada

Fort Edmonton Park T.A.L.E.S. Annual Labor Day Weekend • Edmonton, Alberta, Canada • September • Gail de Vos, 10523 100th Ave., Edmonton, Alberta, Canada T5J 0A8. (403) 424-7764.

Northwest Regional Festival of Puppeteers of America • Vancouver, British Columbia • October • Bev London, 650 Esquimalt, West Vancouver, British Columbia, Canada V7T 1J5.

1,001 Friday Nights of Storytelling • Toronto, Ontario, Canada • Every Friday night • Carol Howe, 412A College St., Toronto, Ontario, Canada M5T 1T3. (416) 924-8625.

Stories Aloud • Baden, Ontario, The Second Story Workshop • First Friday of every month (except August) • Mary-Eileen McClear, 89 Snyders Rd. W., Baden, Ontario, Canada N0B 1G0. (519) 634-8973.

Toronto Festival of Storytelling • Toronto, Ontario • Annually on the last weekend in February • Carol Howe, 412A College St., Toronto, Ontario, Canada M5T 1T3. (416) 924-8625.

Vancouver Children's Festival • Vanier Park, Vancouver, Canada • May • Jackie Asante, CIAYA, #302-601 Cambie St., Vancouver, B.C., Canada V6B 2P1. (604) 687-7697.

Ireland

Siamsa MacManus • Donegal, Ireland • July • Fiountan Gogart/Donegal Craft Village, Donegal County, Donegal, Ireland. Tele 073 22015.

Northern Ireland

Ulster Storytelling Festival, "The Yarnspinners" • Linen Hall Library, Belfast • June • Liz Weir, 38 Lismurns Park, Ahoghill County Antrim, BT 421JN. Northern Ireland (0266) U.K. 871583.

Germany

"Lend me your ears, I've come to tell you a story" • In parks, libraries, and schools in West Germany and abroad • Stefan Kuntz, Maria-Hilf-Strasse 9, D-5000 Koin 1, Federal Republic of Germany, Tele 02 21/ 32 87 58.

California

New Dimensions Newsletter • $35 annually • Published 6 times a year • Justine and Michael Toms, P.O. Box 410510, San Francisco, CA 94141. (415) 563-8899.

Stories: A Western Storytelling Newsletter • $13 annually • Published quarterly • Katy Rydell, 12600 Woodbine St., Los Angeles, CA 90066. (213) 398-3701.

The Story Bag Newsletter • $15 annually • Published monthly • Harlynne Geisler, 5361 Javier S., San Diego, CA 92117. (619) 569-9399.

Storyline • $10 annually • Published quarterly • Kate Frankel, 1 Rochdale Way, Berkeley, CA 94708. (415) 525-1533.

Connecticut

Connecticut Storytelling Newsletter • $15 annually • Published quarterly, distributed through membership in Connecticut Storytelling Center • Nancy Firth, Dept. of Education, Connecticut College, New London, CT 06320. (203) 447-7738.

Florida

Better Telling • $3 annually • Published 3 times a year • Duchess of Magpie, 445 Nelson Dr., Merritt Island, FL 32953. (407) 452-6772.

The Story Times • Benefit of membership in Florida Storytelling Guild, $12 annually • Published quarterly • Florida Storytellers' Guild, P.O. Box 540234, Orlando, FL 32854. (407) 645-3913.

Hawaii

Storytelling Association of Hawaii Newsletter • Distributed bi-monthly as benefit of membership • Roxanne Lawson, P.O. Box 1055, Waianae, HI 96792. (808) 696-4723.

Illinois

Writers/Storytellers Newsletter • $5 annually • Published 6 times a year • Betty Mowery, 1530 7th St., Rock Island, IL 61201. (309) 788-3980.

Indiana

The Story Continues • Benefit of membership in Stories, Inc. $15 annually • Published quarterly • Bob Sander, Stories, Inc., P.O. Box 20743. Indianapolis, IN 46220. (317) 255-7628.

Louisiana

Fairy Tales • $12 annually • Published monthly • Susan H. Glazer, 509 Williams Blvd., Kenner, LA 70062. (504) 465-0550.

Maryland

Phoenix Rising • $25 annually • Published 6 times a year • Diane Finley, Drawer C, Odenton, MD 21113. (301) 674-5323.

Massachusetts

LANES Museletter • $25 L.A.N.E.S. annual membership, $15 subscription (institutions only) • Published 5 times a year • Betty Lehrman, Box

PUBLICATIONS

1483, Arlington, MA 02174. (617) 396-5363.

Minnesota

Storytelling Calendar • Published quarterly • Sarah Meybaum, 3522 Harriet Ave. So. #205, Minneapolis, MN 55408. (612) 825-3965.

Missouri

Gateway Grapevine • $5 annually • Published bi-monthly • Roger Rose, 527 Greeley Ave., Webster Groves, MO 63119. (314) 961-6251.

Midwest Supporters of Storytelling Newsletter • $15 annually • Published quarterly • Vivian Hartzler-Hunt, Midwest Storytelling Theatre, 9100 Cherry, Kansas City, MO 64131. (816) 444-5537.

The MO-TELL Register • Benefit of membership in MO-TELL • Published quarterly • Harriet Lippert, 620 Selma, Webster Groves, MO 63119. (314) 962-4321.

New Jersey

16th Conference Proceedings • Included in registration fee of 16th Children's Literature and Storytelling Conference • Published annually • Eileen Burke and Gwendolyn Jones, Forcina Hall #333, Trenton State College, Hillwood Lakes CN 4700, Trenton, NJ 08650-4700. (609) 771-2465.

Story Art Magazine • Benefit of membership in Garden State Storytellers' League, $16 annually • Published quarterly • Helen Lea, National Story League, c/o Carol Satz, 2100 Lawrenceville Rd., Lawrenceville, NJ 08648. (609) 896-2746.

Yearbook • Benefit of membership in Garden State Storytellers' League, $16 annually • Published annually • Gwendolyn Jones and Carol Satz, 2100 Lawrenceville Rd., Lawrenceville, NJ 08648. (609) 896-2746.

New York

Jewish Storytelling Newsletter • $10 annually • Published 3 times a year

• Peninnah Schram, Jewish Storytelling Center, 92nd St. YM-YWHA Library, 1395 Lexington Ave., New York, NY 10128. (212) 415-5544.

Story Circle Newsletter • $5 annually • Published bi-monthly through membership • Betty McCanty, 31 Columbia Ave., Ballston Spa, NY 12020. (518) 885-4171.

Ohio

OOPS! News • Subscription/membership $15 annually • Published quarterly • Donna Shedlarz, 26 Basin St. N.W., Nevarre, OH 44662. (216) 879-2537.

Story Art Magazine • Benefit of membership in National Story League, $12 annually • Published quarterly • Helen Lea, 555 Tod Ave. N.W., Warren, OH 44485.

Pennsylvania

Storytellers Unlimited • $5 annually • Published monthly • Michael P. Snyder, 228 Glen Springs Ci., Canonsburg, PA 15317. (412) 745-5998.

Patchwork Newsletter • $15 annually • Published bi-monthly • Don La-Branche & Joan Wolff, 518 W. Clapier St., Philadelphia, PA 19144. (215) 849-8783.

Tennessee

Storytelling Magazine • Benefit of NAPPS membership, $25 annually • Published quarterly • Mary Weaver, NAPPS, P.O. Box 309, Jonesborough, TN 37659. (615) 753-2171.

The Tennessee Storytelling Journal • $10 annually, or free with TAPPS membership • Published twice a year • Flora Joy, ETSU, Box 21910A, Johnson City, TN 37614. (615) 929-4297.

Yarnspinner • Benefit of NAPPS Membership PLUS, $40 annually • Published 8 times a year • Mary Weaver, NAPPS, P.O. Box 309, Jonesborough, TN 37659. (615) 753-2171.

Texas

The Oral Bard (Audio Newstape) • $12 annually or free with membership in Houston Storytellers Guild • Published 3 times a year • Bob Graziano, 919 Northwood #5616, Baytown, Texas 77521. (713) 422-4742.

Pass It On! • $10 annually or free with membership in Tejas Storytelling Association • Published 3 times a year • Stacey Emmerick, 110 C. West Oak, Denton, TX 76201. (817) 565-1968

The Texas Teller • $15 annually or free with membership in Tejas Storytelling Association • Published quarterly • Stacey Emmerick, 110 C. West Oak, Denton, TX 76201. (817) 565-1968.

Virginia

Northern Virginia Storyteller • $6 annually • Published quarterly • Joan Leotta, 9728 Stipp St., Burke, VA 22015. (703) 455-4711.

Washington

In the Wind • $10 annually • Published quarterly • Sally Porter-Smith, P.O. Box 45532, Seattle, WA 98145-0532. (206) 621-8646.

Olympia Storytelling Guild Newsletter • $5 individual, $7 family, annually. Free with membership • Published monthly • Rosanne Horovitz, 122 N. Percival, Olympia, WA 98502. (206) 357-9371.

Telling Tales in Schools • $10 annually • Published annually • Cathy Spagnoli, 5646 25th Ave. S.W., Seattle, WA 98106. (206) 937-8679.

Washington, D.C.

Voices in the Glen • Benefit of membership in Voices in the Glen, Ltd., $10 annually, associate membership • Published bi-monthly • Ralph Chatham, Alan Booth, or Paul van Gulick, 2631 Krklyn St., Falls Church, VA 22043. (703) 698-5456.

Wisconsin

Do Tell!—Storytelling Enthusiast's Newsletter • $5 annually • Published semi-annually • Reid Miller, Box 178, Blue Mounds, WI 53517-0178. (608) 437-3388, manager, (608) 437-3440.

Canada

Appleseed • $20 annually • Published 3 times a year • The Storytellers School of Toronto, 412A College St., Toronto, Ontario, Canada M5T 1T3. (416) 924-8625.

Stone Soup Crystals • $3 annually • Published quarterly • Kay Stone, 154 Queenston St., Winnipeg, Manitoba, Canada R3N 0W7. (204) 489-5226.

Taleteller • Free with membership in The Alberta League Encouraging Storytelling (TALES) • Published intermittently • Merle Harris, 10523-100th Ave., Edmonton, Alberta, Canada T5J 0A8. (403) 424-7764.

Arkansas

Petit Jean Storytelling Weekend • Petit Jean State Park, Morrillton, Arkansas • November • Weekend retreat in Arkansas Ozarks. Workshops and individual critiques. Beginning/advanced • Advanced academic credit • Finley Stewart and Jeannine Beekman, Box 441, Krum, TX 76249. (817) 565-1968.

California

Beginners Storytelling Workshop • College of the Desert, Palm Desert, California • Spring and fall semesters • Learning a story, techniques of telling, props, kinds of stories to tell • No credit • Peggy Prentice, 1962 Baristo Rd., Palm Springs, CA 92262. (619) 322-4732.

Beginning and Intermediate Storytell-

EDUCATIONAL OPPORTUNITIES

ing • Flax Vineyard-estate, Healdsburg, California • Summer 1990 • Explore telling: world tales, family stories, original and historical stories. *Safe* environment • Graduate credit • Sandra MacLees, 6695 Westside Rd., Healdsburg, CA 95448. (707) 433-8728.

Bringing Biblical Humor and Story to Life • Pacific School of Religion, Berkeley, California and Bay Area • July • Story, drama, clown, mime with Margie Brown, Ed Stivender, Diane Ferlott, others • Graduate credit, CEUs • Carol Voisin, Pacific School of Religion, 1798 Scenic Ave., Berkeley, CA 94709. (415) 848-0528.

Dominican College Certificate-in-Storytelling Program • Dominican College, San Rafael, California • Year-round • Credit and non-credit classes offered evenings and weekends for all levels • CEUs • Ruth Stotter, 1520 Grand Ave., San Rafael, CA 94901. (415) 485-3255.

Laura Simms Annual Storytelling Residency • Wellspring Renewal Center, Philo, California • August • In-depth performance lab in all aspects of storytelling: master classes, voice, movement, and study • Undergraduate credit • Todd Evans, Wellspring Renewal Center, Box 332, Philo, CA, 95466. (707) 895-3893.

Storytelling Classes • San Jose State University, Monterrey, California Regional Festival • Year-round • Courses in beginning and advanced and symposium storytelling for teachers, librarians • CEUs, undergraduate credit • Bob Jenkins, Theatre Arts—SJSU, San Jose, CA 95192. (408) 924-4536.

Storytelling Classes • University of San Diego • Spring, Fall • The spring 3-unit course includes class, workshops, and four concerts • Fall semester course offering by the Storytellers of San Diego • Graduate credit • Vicky Reed, 1840 W. Montecito Way, San Diego, CA 92103. (619) 298-6363.

Storytelling Workshop • San Diego, California • Spring and Fall • Workshops for beginning, intermediate, and teacher storytellers • No credit • Harlynne Geisler, 5361 Javier St., San Diego, CA 92117. (619) 569-9399.

Storytelling Workshop with Olga Loya • Eureka, California • Dates to be announced • Learn techniques on how to find your life stories and tell them • No credit • Olga Loya, P.O. Box 6766, Eureka, CA 95501. (707) 442-4228.

The Wilden Workshop • Cedar Mountain, North Carolina • August • Five-day storytelling retreat led by Milbre Burch features critiques and movement study • No credit • Milbre Burch, Kind Crone Productions, 582 Eldora Rd., Pasadena, CA 91104. (818) 797-6817.

A Workshop in Personal Presence for Storytellers • Domenican College, San Rafael, California • Carolyn Power, Domenican College, 1520 Grand Ave., San Rafael, CA 94901. (415) 485-3255, or (415) 752-1431.

Connecticut

Storytelling Confratute • University of Connecticut, Storrs, Connecticut • July • Teachers learn storytelling skills and how to train students to be storytellers • Graduate credit • Dr. Gail N. Herman, Route 2, Lodge Circle, Swanton, MD 21561. (203) 486-4826.

Colorado

Storytelling for Everyone • University of Colorado, Boulder, Colorado • Monday nights in April • Discovery and communication of individuals' unique styles and how to present them • No credit • Kay Negash, 5445 White Pl., Boulder, CO 80303. (303) 447-8679.

Rocky Mountain Storytelling Festival Workshops • Palmer Lake, Colorado • August • Informative workshops for beginners and experienced tellers • Graduate/undergraduate credit • John Stansfield, Box 588, Monument, CO 80132. (719) 481-3202.

Florida

Florida Storytelling Camp • Camp Moon, Leesburg, Florida • March • 3-day participation workshops and evening performances featuring national and Florida storytellers • CEUs • Florida Storytellers' Guild, P.O. Box 540234, Orlando, FL 32854. (407) 645-3913.

Talebearing: The Art of Storytelling • Temple Beth Or, Miami, Florida • March • An introduction to the techniques of storytelling and improvisation for novice storytellers • No credit • Rabbi Rami M. Shapiro, Temple Beth Or, P.O. Box 160081, Miami, FL 33116. (305) 235-1419.

Georgia

Stovall House Retreat • Helen, Georgia • September • Weekend retreat for current issues of fledgling and advanced storytellers • No credit • Fiona Page, 1270 Woodstream Dr., Lawrenceville, GA 30244. (404) 381-7888.

Young Harris Education Conference • Young Harris College, Young Harris, Georgia • Educational retreat for librarians and teachers on using storytelling in the classroom • No credit • Fiona Page, 1270 Woodstream Dr., Lawrenceville, GA 30244. (404) 381-7888.

Illinois

Storytelling Course • Northwestern University, Evanston, Illinois • July • Storytelling as a bridge to content areas in the classroom, elsewhere • Course also to be taught at University of Missouri in St. Louis, Missouri, and at two Wisconsin sites for Viterbo College, La Crosse, Wisconsin • Graduate credit • Rives Collins, 1979 Sheridan Rd., Evanston, IL 60208. (708) 491-5250.

Storytelling • Sangamon State University, Springfield, Illinois • Spring semester • Upper division course in storytelling performance and literature • Graduate/undergraduate credit • Dr. David Hilligoss, Sanga-

mon State University, Springfield, IL 62708. (217) 786-6789.

Louisiana

Fairy Special Fantasy Festivals • The Fantasy Cottage, Kenner, Louisiana • Held monthly, as needed • How to tell a story to a child, for parents, storytellers, teachers. • No credit • Jane S. Kreisman, 509 Williams Blvd., Kenner, LA 70062. (504) 464-1410.

Maryland

Storytelling Apprenticeship with Milbre Burch • John Carroll University, Cleveland, Ohio • July • Intensive, small-group setting, extended master class, daily critique, special classes, field trips • CEUs • Jorja Davis, Phoenix, Drawer C, Odenton, MD 21113. (301) 674-5323.

Storytelling: A Tapestry of Talent • Frostburg State University, Frostburg, Maryland • June • Teachers learn storytelling skills and how to train students to be storytellers • Graduate credit • Dr. Gail N. Herman, Rte. 2 Lodge Circle, Swanton, MD 21561. (301) 387-9199.

Massachusetts

Judith Black and Doug Lipman: Telling Stories to Children • Marblehead, Massachusetts • June • Doug and Judith lead participants in four days of workshops, coaching, and tellings • Judith Black, 33 Prospect St., Marblehead, MA 01945. (617) 631-4417.

Making Fairy Tales from Personal Stories with Doug Lipman • Winchester, Massachusetts • August • Telling difficult, confidential personal stories through fairy tale symbols and structures • No credit • Doug Lipman, P.O. Box 441195, W. Somerville, MA 02144. (617) 391-3672.

Oak and Stone Storytelling • Worcester/Princeton, Massachusetts • Winter, spring, and fall • Storytelling workshop, 6 sessions, for beginning and/or experienced storytellers • No credit • Katie Green or Cheryl Savageau, P.O. Box 1212, Worcester, MA 01613. (508) 464-5146.

Storytelling from the Inside-Out • The Studio—Oak Bluffs, Island of Martha's Vineyard, Massachusetts • July • Intensive. Connecting to stories inside. Positive critiques, "Klein method." Limited to 6 • No credit • Susan Klein, Box 214, Oak Bluffs, MA 02557. (508) 693-4140.

Storytelling Workshops • Western Massachusetts • One-day and weekend workshops. Beginning and advanced skills, personal and family storytelling • CEUs • Robert Harris, 12 Westview Dr., Belchertown, MA 01007. (413) 323-6121.

Telling Stories to Children with Doug Lipman and Judith Black • Marblehead, Massachusetts • June • How to tell stories to children and help children tell their stories • No credit • Doug Lipman, P.O. Box 441195, W. Somerville, MA 02144. (617) 391-3672.

Winter Weekend of Storytelling • Point Way Inn, Edgartown, Massachusetts • January • Susan Klein telling and teaching for beginners, professionals. Participants stay at Inn • No credit • Linda Smith, Point Way Inn, Edgartown, MA 02539. (508) 627-8633.

Women's Storytelling Intensive • Martha's Vineyard, Massachusetts • March • Extended master class for women only. Taught by two gifted teller-teachers • No credit • Susan Klein and Milbre Burch, Box 214, Oak Bluffs, MA 02557. (508) 693-4140.

Michigan

Graduate Level Course in Storytelling • Wayne State University, Detroit • Offered once a year for semester • Basic skills in selecting, preparing, and delivering stories orally • Graduate credit • R. Craig Rooney, 287 Education, Wayne State University, Detroit, MI 48202. (313) 577-0928.

Storytelling in Education Conference • Holiday Inn in Saginaw, Lansing, Michigan • May • Includes an evening of storytelling • No credit • Sharon Horgon, Office of Continuing Education, Rowe 125, Central Michigan University, Mt. Pleasant, MI 48859. (517) 774-3718.

Minnesota

Storytelling and Folklore • Metro State University, Minneapolis–St. Paul, Minnesota • Spring and fall quarter • Storytelling course featuring all traditional and literary styles • Undergraduate credit • Elaine Wynn, Metro State University, 7th and Robert St., Minneapolis, MN 55101. (612) 296-3875.

Storytelling as a Modern Communication Art • Metro State University, Minneapolis–St. Paul, Minnesota • Winter quarter • Structuring and telling personal stories for all occupational disciplines • Undergraduate credit • Larry Johnson and Elaine Wynne, 2615 S. 6th St., Minneapolis, MN 55454. (612) 333-0970.

Mississippi

Workshop • Braden School, Natchez, Mississippi • September • Featured Magnolia Storytelling Festival tellers offer workshops on a variety of topics • Berry G. Bateman, 201 Dunbarton, Natchez, MS 39120. (601) 442-9407.

Missouri

Storytelling Class • School of the Ozarks, Point Lookout, Missouri • Spring semester • The art, methods, techniques, and practice of selecting, adapting, and telling stories • Undergraduate credit • Jean Smith, Library, School of the Ozarks, Point Lookout, MO 65726. (417) 334-6411.

Workshop • University of Missouri–St. Louis • February • Belden Lane, Elaine Wynne, Larry Johnson. Metaphor—*Healing Everyday Life with Storytelling* • No credit • Nan Kammann, UM St. Louis, 8001 Natural Bridge Rd., St. Louis, MO 63121. (314) 553-5911.

Workshops • University of Missouri–St. Louis • May. Free workshops as part of St. Louis Storytelling Festival • No credit • Nan Kammann, University of Missouri–St. Louis, 8001 Natural Bridge Rd., St. Louis, MO 63121. (314) 553-5911.

Storytelling Classes • University of Missouri–St. Louis • June and July • Lynn Rubright's storytelling course • Graduate/undergraduate credit • Brenda Shannon, University of Missouri–St. Louis, 8001 Natural Bridge Rd., St. Louis, MO 63121. (314) 553-5911.

Storytelling Course • University of Missouri • June–July • Storytelling as a bridge to content areas in the classroom, elsewhere • Graduate credit • Rives Collins, 1979 Sheridan Rd., Evanston, IL 60208. (708) 491-5250.

Storytelling Intensive • Arrow Rock State Historic Site, Arrow Rock, Missouri • Last week of July • Vocal and physical characterization, quick learn and creative activities • Graduate and undergraduate credit, CEUs • Susan Sylvia Scott, 9100 Cherry, Kansas City, MO 64131. (810) 444-5537.

New Jersey

The Magic of Storytelling • Princeton University, Princeton, New Jersey • August • Week-long storytelling residency with Susan Danoff and guest artists • No credit • Susan Danoff, 117 Gedney Rd., Lawrenceville, NJ 08648. (609) 882-2879.

National Story League Convention • Princeton Marriott Hotel, Princeton, New Jersey • July • Join the group that provides "service through storytelling" for workshops, storytelling, fellowship • No credit • Dr. Gwendolyn Jones, 635 E. Third St., Florence, NJ 08518.

Storytelling Course • Rutgers University, New Brunswick, New Jersey • June–July • Basic course in storytelling designed for librarians and teachers who work with children • Graduate credit • Ellin Greene and Betty Turock, Rutgers University SCILS, 4 Huntington St., New Brunswick, NJ 08903. (201) 932-7917.

Whole Theatre School • Whole Theatre, Montclair, New Jersey • On-going • Storytelling and story-theatre workshops for beginning and experienced tellers • No credit • Gerald Fierst, 544 Bloomfield Ave., Montclair, NJ 07042. (201) 744-2933.

New York

Stories from the Heart • New York, New York • February • Giving ourselves permission to succeed as tellers. Activity, lecture, and performance format • No credit • Susan Klein, Box 214, Oak Bluffs, MA 02557. (508) 693-4140.

North Carolina

The Art of Storytelling • Rowan-Cabarrus Community College, Salisbury, North Carolina • On-going • College class • Undergraduate credit, CEUs • Alisha Sides Wilson, Rowan-Cabarrus Community College, P.O. Box 1595, Salisbury, NC 28145-9985. (704) 782-6000.

Children's Literature and Storytelling • University of North Carolina at Greensboro • Spring and fall semesters • On-going • Traditional and multi-ethnic literature, family history as story, basic storytelling skills • Undergraduate credit • Barbara Moran, 1102 Spring Garden St., Greensboro, NC 27403. (919) 274-7082.

Ohio

Jewish Storytelling Conference • Ohio State University, Columbus, Ohio • August • Jewish storytelling workshops, performance as part of major Jewish education conference • No credit • Peninnah Schram, 525

West End Ave., Apt. 8C, New York, NY 10024. (212) 787-0626.

Tell Me a Story—Storytelling as a Prevention Strategy in the Classroom • Ohio and contiguous states • Date to be arranged • For those working with children K-6, provides tool for conveying information, skills • No credit • Guenveur H. Burnell, 600 Edgewood Dr., Kent, OH 44240. (216) 673-0585.

Zanesville Storytelling Masters Class • Zanesville Center, Ohio University, Zanesville, Ohio • June • Workshop for experienced storytellers led by Mary Hamilton and Marcia Lane • Graduate/undergraduate credit • David Mitzel, Ohio University–Zanesville Center, 1425 Newark Rd., Zanesville, OH 43701. (614) 453-0762.

Oregon

Storytelling Class • Southwestern Oregon Community College, Coos Bay, Oregon and throughout Coos/Curry County • Dates by request • Five-week intensive explores aspects of creativity in storytelling. Class content varies • No credit • Rachel Foxman, P.O. Box 1663, Bandon, OR 97411. (503) 347-2188.

Storyteller Retreat • Medford, Oregon • August • A mentor workshop with Barbara Griffin. Professional techniques for your storytelling journey • Barbara Budge Griffin, 10 S. Keeneway Dr., Medford, OR 97504. (503) 773-3006.

Tennessee

Master's Degree in Storytelling/Reading • East Tennessee State University, Johnson City, Tennessee • Ongoing • Courses available to special enrollees and those not pursuing a degree • Graduate/undergraduate credit • Dr. Flora C. Joy, ETSU, Box 21910A, Johnson City, TN 37614. (615) 929-4260.

National Storytelling Institute • Jonesborough, Tennessee • May–August • A selection of short courses in the storytelling art • Graduate/under-graduate credit • NAPPS, P.O. Box 309, Jonesborough, TN 37659. (615) 753-2171.

Texas

Workshops • The Houston Storytellers Guild • Beginning workshop—fall, specialized workshop—spring • Armand Bayou Tale Tellin' Festival workshops, May • CEUs available at festival • Sally Goodroe or Jim Ohmart, 1525 W. Main St. #4, Houston, TX 77006. (713) 523-3289 or 674-2528.

Vermont

Vermont Storytelling Festival • Church Street Center and Fletcher Free Library, Burlington, Vermont • November • Ten 90-minute workshops and six public performances featuring fifteen area tellers • No credit • Peter Burns, 205 King St., Burlington, VT 05401. (802) 658-3659.

Virginia

Busch Gardens Storytelling Festival • Busch Gardens, The Old Country, Williamsburg, Virginia • May • Workshops and special teacher's guide available to educational groups with advance registration • No credit • Busch Gardens Storytelling Festival, Group Sales Dept., One Busch Blvd., Williamsburg, VA 23187-8785. (804) 253-3350.

Eve Watters' Storytelling Workshop • Children's Bookshop, Charlottesville, Virginia • April 1 and September • Light your tale-telling fire. Lively workout for adults of all experience levels • No credit • Eve Watters, P.O. Box 1792, Charlottesville, VA 22902. (804) 296-1408.

Interdisciplinary Performance Through Storytelling • KI Theatre and Arts Center, Washington, Virginia • July • Develop new performance work based on stories with Julie Portman, workshop staff • No credit • Julie Portman, KI Theatre, P.O. Box 203, Washington, VA 22747. (703) 987-3164.

Telling for Teachers • Fairfax, Virginia (or your site) • February and August annually and as requested • Training in story techniques and applications for math, science, social science, language arts • No credit • Joan Leotta, 9728 Stipp St., Burke, VA 22015. (703) 455-4711.

Washington

Storytelling for Everyone • Seattle, Washington • Offered quarterly through University of Washington's Experimental College • Introductory course to develop storytelling confidence and beginning repertoire • No credit • Cathryn Wellner, 1947 14th Ave. E., Seattle, WA 98112. (206) 328-1328.

Storytelling for Educators • Pacific Lutheran University, Tacoma, Washington • July–August • Practical course designed to give K-12 teachers confidence in storytelling skills • Graduate credit • Cathryn Wellner, 1947 14th E., Seattle, WA 98112. (206) 328-1328.

Teaching with Tales: Storytelling for Educators • Seattle Pacific University • Spring quarter • Storytelling for educators. Build confidence, repertoire, storytelling, and puppetry skills • Graduate credits • Naomi Baltuck, P.O. Box 836, Edmonds, WA 98020. (206) 776-1175.

Washington, D.C.

The Art of Storytelling • The American University, Washington, D.C. • May–June • Course for novice tellers: improvisation, developing stories, performance, analysis of tales • Graduate/undergraduate credit • Jo Radner, Department of Literature, American University, Washington, D.C., 20016. (202) 885-2982.

Wisconsin

Summer Storytelling Course • University of Wisconsin, Milwaukee • June–July • Storytelling course emphasizing forms of storytelling true to their original culture base • Graduate/undergraduate credit • Wilfred Fong or Anne Pellowski, P.O. Box 413 UW-M, Milwaukee, WI 53201. (414) 229-4709.

Storytelling Course • Viterbo College, La Crosse, Wisconsin • June, August • Storytelling as a bridge to content areas in the classroom, elsewhere. Graduate credit • Rives Collins, 1979 Sheridan Rd., Evanston, IL 60208. (708) 491-5250.

Canada

Courses, Workshops, and Summer School • Toronto, Canada • Schedule mailed on request • Introductory and advanced courses, workshops for working tellers, 4-day intensive summer session • No credit, completion certificate provided • Carol Howe, 412A College St., Toronto, Ontario, Canada M5T 1T3. (416) 924-8625.

International Symposium on Arts for Young Audiences • On-site at the Vancouver Children's Festival, Vancouver, Canada • May 18–21, 1990 • Brings artists, educators, presenters, and delegates together to discuss topics of importance • Norma Laidlaw, CIAYA, #302, 601 Cambie St., Vancouver, British Columbia, Canada V6B 2P1. (604) 687-7697.

Techniques of Storytelling • University of Winnipeg, Winnipeg, Canada • Fall term • Introduces new tellers to storytelling through participation exercises • Undergraduate credit • Kay Stone, English Dept., Univ. of Winnipeg, Winnipeg, Manitoba, Canada R3B 2E9. (204) 786-9497.

Scotland

Storytelling Workshop • Forres, Moray, Scotland • November 10–16, 1990 • Storytelling as meditation with Peter Vallance • No credit • Workshops Focauser, Newbold House, Findhorn Foundation, St., Leonards Rd., Forres, Moray, Scotland IV36 ORE. Tele 0309 72659.

Venezuela

Storytelling Techniques and Uses in Education and Social Development • Caracas, Venezuela • Twice a year • Develop telling capabilities and uses in education and social development • No credit • Daniel Mato, Magdamar (9-A). Av. Ppal. Santa Fe Sur, Caracas-1080, Venezuela. 979-8448.

Research Seminar on Traditional Forms of Storytelling • Various Universities in Venezuela • Ongoing • Daniel Mato, Magdamar (9-A). Av. Ppal. Santa Fe Sur, Caracas-1080, Venezuela. 979-8448.

CALENDAR

January

ALA Storytelling Discussion Group, Chicago, IL

Olde Christmas Storytelling Festival, Atlanta, GA

Winter Weekend of Storytelling, Edgartown, MA

February

Northwest Storytelling Festival, Seattle, WA

Stories from the Heart, New York, NY

Telling for Teachers, Fairfax, VA

Toronto Festival of Storytelling, Toronto, Ontario

Wild Onion Storytelling Celebration, Winnetka, IL

Workshop, University of Missouri, St. Louis, MO

March

Cherry Blossom Storytelling Concert, Macon, GA

Storytelling, San Francisco, CA

Florida Storytelling Camp, Leesburg, FL

Mariposa County Storytelling Festival, Mariposa, CA

Sharing the Fire '90, Boston, MA

Talebearing: The Art of Storytelling, Miami, FL

Tapestry of Talent Student Storytelling Festival, Frostburg, MD

Texas Storytelling Festival, Denton, TX

Women's Storytelling Intensive, Martha's Vineyard, MA

April

A(ugusta) Baker's Dozen, Columbia, SC

Atlanta Storytelling Festival, Atlanta, GA

Artsplosure Spring Arts Festival, Raleigh, NC

Bayside Yarnspinners Festival, Mobile, AL

Blossom Time Storytelling Festival, Lake Springfield, IL

Cocoa, Florida Storyfest '90, Merritt Island, FL

Connecticut Storytelling Festival, New London, CT

Eve Watters' Storytelling Workshop, Charlottesville, VA

Folktales for a Fools Day, Harlem, NY

The Gathering, with Lucille Breneman, HI

MO-TELL Storytelling Weekend, Lake of the Ozarks, MO

Piedmont Storytelling Festival, Greensboro/High Point, NC

Storytelling Concert, Scottsdale, AZ

Storytelling for Everyone, Boulder, CO

May

Armand Bayou Tale Tellin' Festival, Houston, TX

The Art of Storytelling, Washington, D.C.

Busch Gardens Storytelling Festival, Williamsburg, VA

Connecticut Student Storytelling Festival, Middletown, CT

Dayton Storytelling Festival, Dayton, OH

International Symposium on Arts for Young Audiences, Vancouver

National Storytelling Institute, Jonesborough, TN

Ohio State Storytelling Festival (OOPS!), Chesterville, OH

Renaissance City Storyfest, Detroit, MI

Southern California Storyswapping Festival, San Diego, CA

Storytelling in Education Conference, Lansing, MI

Troupe of Tellers, Eugene, Oregon

Vancouver Children's Festival, Vancouver, B.C., Canada

Washington Storytelling Festival, Glen Echo, MD

Workshop, St. Louis Storytelling Festival, St. Louis, MO

June

ALA Storytelling Discussion Group, Chicago, IL

Big Apple Storytelling Festival, New York, NY

Big Woods Storytelling Festival, Nerstrand State Park, MN

Judith Black and Doug Lipman: Telling Stories to Children, Marblehead, MA

Mid-Atlantic/Northeast Regional Festival, Puppeteers of America, Bryn Mawr, PA

National Congress on Storytelling, Minneapolis–St. Paul, MN

National Storytelling Institute, Jonesborough, TN

Storytelling Course, La Crosse, WI

Storytelling Course, New Brunswick, NJ

Storytelling Course, St. Louis, MO

Storytelling: A Tapestry of Talent, Frostburg, MD

Summer Solstice Folk Music & Dance Festival, Northridge, CA

Summer Storytelling, Milwaukee, WI

SunFest Storytelling Festival, Barlesville, OK

Super-Duper Summer Storytelling Festival, Miami, FL

TAPPS Storytelling Festival, Memphis, TN

Telling Stories to Children, Marblehead, MA

Third Festival of Storytelling, Oak Bluffs, MA

Ulster Storytelling Festival, Belfast, N. Ireland

Vineyard, Oak Bluffs, MA

Zanesville Storytelling Masters Class, Zanesville, OH

July

Bix Storytelling Festival, Davenport, IA

Bringing Biblical Humor and Story to Life, Berkeley, CA

Create, International Conference, Cleveland, OH

Great Lakes Regional Festival, Puppeteers of America, Schaumburg, IL

Great Plains Regional Festival, Puppeteers of America, Kansas City, MO

Illinois Storytelling Festival, Spring Grove, IL

Interdisciplinary Performance Through Storytelling, Washington, VA

Iowa Storytelling Festival, Clear Lake, IA

Long Island Summer Storytelling Festival, Sayville, NY

Mid-Atlantic Storytellers Gathering, Millersville, PA

National Story League Convention, Princeton, NJ

National Storytelling Institute, Jonesborough, TN

Riverside Tales Festival, Manhattan, NY

Siamsa MacManus, Donegal, Ireland

Sierra Storytelling Festival, Nevada City, CA

Storytelling Apprenticeship with Milbre Burch, Cleveland, OH

Storytelling Classes, St. Louis, MO

Storytelling Confratute, Storrs, CT

Storytelling Course, Evanston, IL

Storytelling for Educators, Tacamo, WA

Storytelling from the Inside-Out, Martha's Vineyard, MA

Storytelling Intensive, Arrow Rock, MO

August

Biblical Storytelling Workshop, Alexandra, MN

Hoosier Storytelling Festival, Indianapolis, IN

Jewish Storytelling Conference, Columbus, OH

Laura Simms Annual Storytelling Residency, Philo, CA

The Magic of Storytelling, Princeton, NJ

Making Fairy Tales from Personal

Stories with Doug Lipman, Winchester, MA

Pacific Southwest Regional Festival, Puppeteers of America, Berkeley, CA

Rocky Mountain Storytelling Festival Workshop, Palmer Lake, CO

Scotts Mill Storytelling Festival, Scotts, MI

Second Rocky Mountain Storytelling Festival, Palmer Lake, CO

Southeast Regional Festival, Puppeteers of America, Helen, GA

Storyteller Retreat, Medford, OR

Telling for Teachers, Fairfax, VA

Wilder Workshop, Cedar Mountain, NC

September

Artsplosure Autumn Jazz and Heritage Festival, Raleigh, NC

Cedar River Storytelling Festival, Waverly, IO

Eve Watters' Storytelling Workshop, Charlottesville, VA

Fall Storytelling Festival, Raleigh, NC

Fort Edmonton Park, Edmonton, Alberta, CA

Jonnycake Storytelling Festival, Peace Dale, RI

Magnolia Storytelling Festival, Natchez, MS

Northwest Region Puppeteers of America Regional Festival, Vancouver, B.C., Canada

Stovall House Retreat, Helen, GA

Tales Told Under an Apple Tree: Storyfests, Bethel, CT

Talking Island Festival, Honolulu, HI

Zanesville Storyfest, Zanesville, OH

Workshop, Natchez, MS

October

End of Summer Celebration, Merritt Island, FL

Ghost Stories at Clayville, Springfield, IL

Ghost Stories by Riverbend Storytelling Guild, Moline, IL

Halloween Ghost Storytelling Festival, Mt. Horeb, WI

Halloween Storyfest, Johnson City, TN

ILA Storytellers Roundtable, IO

Live Oak Storytelling Festival, Charleston, SC

M.A.S.T. (Milwaukee Area Story Tellers Guild), Milwaukee, WI

MO-TELL Storytelling Weekend, Troy, MI

National Storytelling Festival™, Jonesborough, TN

Northwest Regional Festival of Puppeteers of America, Vancouver, BC

Pumpkin Patch Festival, Wyckoff, NJ

Sixteenth Children's Literature Festival, Trenton, NJ

Storytelling '90, Dearborn, MI

Tales Told Under an Apple Tree: Storyfests, Bethel, CT

Talking Island Festival, Honolulu, HI

Three Apples Storytelling Festival, Harvard, MA

November

Children's Book Week, Lafayette, LA

Elva Young Van Winkle Storytelling Festival, Washington, D.C.

Petit Jean Storytelling Weekend, Morrillton, AR

POPO Puppet Festival, Iowa City, IO

Storyfest '90, Norwich, NY

Storytelling Workshop, Forres, Moray, Scotland

Tellabration Texas!, Texas

Vermont Storytelling Festival, Burlington, VT

Seasonal

Beginners Storytelling Workshop, Palm Desert, CA

Beginning and Intermediate Storytelling, Healdsburg, CA

Graduate Level Course in Storytelling, Detroit, MI

Humboldt Storytellers, Arcata, CA

Jackson and Friends, Mt. Desert, ME

Modern Communication, Storytelling as an Art, Minneapolis, MN

National Storytelling Institute, Jonesborough, TN

Oak and Stone Storytelling, Worcester/Princeton, MA

Puppet Showplace Theatre, Brighton, MA

Storytelling and Folklore, Minneapolis, MN

Storytelling Class, Point Lookout, MO

Storytelling Classes, San Diego, CA

Storytelling Discussion Group, Association for Library Service to Children, Chicago, IL

Storytelling, Springfield, IL

Storytelling Techniques and Uses in Education and Social Development, Caracas, Venezuela

Storytelling Workshop, San Diego, CA

Teaching with Tales—Storytelling for Educators, Seattle, WA

Techniques of Storytelling, Winnipeg, Canada

Whole Theatre School, Montclair, NJ

Winter Tales Series, Nevada City, CA

Workshop, Houston, TX

Ongoing

The Art of Storytelling, Salisbury, NC

At the Boiserie, Seattle, WA

By Word of Mouth, Pasadena, CA

Childrens Literature and Storytelling, Greensboro, NC

Community Storytellers, Santa Monica, CA

Dominican College Certificate-In-Storytelling Program, San Rafael, CA

Fairy Special Fantasy Festivals, Kenner, LA

Family Radio Storytelling Program, Santa Barbara, CA

The Fantasy College, Kenner, LA

Jewish Storytelling Center, New York, NY

Lend me your ears, I've come to tell you a story, F.R. of Germany

Masters Degree in Storytelling/Reading, Johnson City, TN

Monthly Story Swap Sessions, Ft. Myers, FL

New York City Storytelling Center Workshops, New York, NY

1001 Friday Nights of Storytelling, Toronto, Ontario, Canada

Research Seminar on Traditional Forms of Storytelling, Venezuela

Salt of the Earth: A Biblical Storytelling Circle, New Hope, MN

Stories After Dark, Brookline, MA

Stories Aloud, Baden, Ontario

Storytellers in Concert Storytelling Concert Series, Cambridge, MA

Storytelling Classes, San Jose, CA

Storytelling for Adults, Minneapolis, MN

Storytelling for Everyone, Seattle, WA

Storytelling Potlucks, Santa Cruz, CA

Storytelling Workshops, Western, MA

Unscheduled

Courses, Workshops, and Summer School, Toronto, Canada

Storytelling Class, Coos Bay, OR

Storytelling Workshop with Olga Loyla, Eureka, CA

Tell Me a Story: Storytelling as a Prevention Strategy in the Classroom, OH

Workshop in Personal Presence for Storytellers, San Rafael, CA

Young Harris Educational Conference, Young Harris, GA

BIBLIOGRAPHY

Books

Abrams, Jeremiah, ed. *Reclaiming the Inner Child*. Los Angeles: Jeremy P. Tarcher, 1990.

Arthur, Stephen, and Arthur, Julia. *Your Life and Times*. Nobleton, Fla.: Heritage Tree Press, 1986.

Bagley, Michael. *Using Imagery in Creative Problem Solving*. Monroe, N.Y.: Trillium Press, 1987.

Bagley, Michael, and Hess, Karin. *Two Hundred Ways of Using Imagery in the Classroom*. Monroe, N.Y.: Trillium Press, 1984.

Baker, Augusta, and Greene, Ellin. *Storytelling Art and Technique*. New York: R. R. Bowker, 1987.

Bell, Corydon. *John Rattling Gourd of Big Cove*. New York: Macmillan, 1955.

Berry, Thomas, *The Dream of the Earth*. San Francisco: Sierra Club Books, 1988.

Biffle, Christopher, *A Journey Through Your Childhood*. Los Angeles: Jeremy P. Tarcher, 1989.

Bly, Robert. *A Little Book on the Human Shadow*. San Francisco: Harper & Row Publishers, Inc., 1988.

Bolen, Jean Shinoda. *Goddesses in Everywoman*. San Francisco: Harper & Row, 1987.

———. *Gods in Everyman*. San Francisco: Harper & Row, 1989.

Bosnak, Robert. *A Little Course in Dreams*. Boston: Shambhala Publications, 1986.

Botkin, Andrew. *Botkin's Treasury of American Folklore*. New York: Crown Publishers, 1950.

Brett, Doris. *Annie Stories*. New York: Workman Publishing, 1986.

Caduto, Michael J., and Bruchac, Joseph. *Keepers of the Earth*. Golden, Colo.: Fulcrum, 1988.

Calder, Nigel. *Timescale: An Atlas of the Fourth Dimension*. New York: Viking Press, 1983.

Campbell, Joseph. *The Hero with a Thousand Faces*. Princeton: Princeton University Press, 1949.

———. *The Inner Reaches of Outer Space*. Toronto: St. James Press, 1986.

———. *The Mythic Image*. Princeton: Princeton University Press, 1974.

———. *Myths to Live By*. New York: Bantam Books, 1988.

———. *The Portable Jung*. New York: Viking Penguin, 1971.

———. *The Power of Myth*. New York: Doubleday, 1988.

Capacchione, Lucia. *The Creative Journal for Children*. Boston: Shambhala Publications, 1982.

Chinen, Allan B. *In the Ever After: Fairy Tales and the Second Half of Life*. Wilmette, Ill.: Chiron Publications, 1989.

Colman, Arthur, and Coleman, Libby. *The Father: Mythology and Changing Roles*. Wilmette, Ill.: Chiron Publications, 1988.

Crystal, John C. and Bolles, Richard, N. *Where Do I Go from Here with My Life?* New York: Seabury Press, 1974.

Doore, Gary, ed. *Shaman's Path*. Boston: Shambhala Publications, 1988.

Eisler, Riane. *The Chalice and the*

Blade. New York: Harper & Row Publishers, 1987.

Eliade, Mircea. *Shamanism.* Princeton, Princeton University Press, 1964.

Elkind, David. *The Hurried Child.* Reading, Mass.: Addison-Wesley, 1981.

Feinstein, David, and Krippner, Stanley. *Personal Mythology.* Los Angeles: Jeremy P. Tarcher, 1988.

Feldmann, Susan. *The Storytelling Stone.* New York: Dell, 1965.

Greene, Ellin, and Shannon, George. *Storytelling: A Selected Annotated Bibliography.* New York: Garland Publishing, 1986.

Grimm, Jacob, and Grimm, Wilhelm. *The Complete Grimm's Fairy Tales.* New York: Random House, 1972.

Guss, David M. *The Language of the Birds: Tales, Texts, and Poems of Interspecies Communication.* Berkeley: North Point Press, 1985.

Haddon, Genia Pauli. *Body Metaphors.* New York: Crossroad Publishing Co., 1988.

Hannah, Barbara. *Encounters with the Soul: Active Imagination.* Boston: Sigo Press, 1981.

Harner, Michael. *The Way of the Shaman.* New York: Bantam Books, 1980.

Hawking, Stephen W. *A Brief History of Time.* New York: Bantam Books, 1988.

Hillman, James. *Children's Literature: The Great Excluded.* Philadelphia: Temple University Press, 1974.

———. *Healing Fiction.* Barrytown, N.Y.: Station Hill Press, 1983.

Houston, Jean. *The Possible Human.* Los Angeles: Jeremy P. Tarcher, 1982.

———. *The Search for the Beloved.* Los Angeles: Jeremy P. Tarcher, 1987.

Johnson, Robert. *He: Understanding Masculine Psychology.* King of Prussia, Pa.: Religious Publishing Co., 1974.

———. *She: Understanding Feminine Psychology.* King of Prussia, Pa.: Religious Publishing Co., 1976.

———. *We: Understanding the Psychology of Romantic Love.* New York: Harper & Row, 1983.

Jung, Carl. *Memories, Dreams, Reflections.* New York: Random House, 1961.

Kalweit, Holger. *Dreamtime and Inner Space: The World of the Shaman.* Boston: Shambhala Publications, 1988.

Livo, Norma J., and Rietz, Sandra A. *Storytelling: Process and Practice.* Littleton, Colo.: Libraries Unlimited, 1986.

Lovelock, James. *The Ages of Gaia.* New York: W. W. Norton, 1988.

———. *Gaia: A New Look at Life on Earth.* New York: Oxford University Press, 1979.

Luthi, Max. *The European Folktale.* Bloomington, Ind.: Indiana University Press, 1982.

———. *Once upon a Time: On the Nature of Fairy Tales.* Bloomington, Ind.: Indiana University Press, 1976.

MacDonald, Margaret Read. *The Storyteller's Sourcebook.* Detroit, Mich.: Gale Research Co., 1982.

Macy, Joanna. *Despair and Personal Power in the Nuclear Age.* Philadelphia: New Society Publishers, 1983.

Maguire, Jack. *Creative Storytelling.* New York: McGraw-Hill, 1985.

Matthews, Caitlin, and Matthews, John. *The Western Way.* Boston: Arkana, 1985.

Moore, Robin. *The Bread Sister of Sinking Creek.* New York: HarperCollins, 1990.

———. *Maggie among the Seneca.* New York: HarperCollins, 1990.

Morris, Richard. *Time's Arrows.* New York: Simon and Schuster, 1985.

Murdock, Maureen. *Spinning Inward: Using Guided Imagery with Children for Learning, Creativity, and Relaxation.* Boston: Shambhala Publications, 1987.

Murphy, Joseph. *The Power of Your Subconscious Mind.* Englewood Cliffs, N.J.: Prentice-Hall, 1963.

Newman, Frederick R. *Mouthsounds.* New York: Workman, 1980.

Nicholson, Shirley. *Shamanism.*

Wheaton, Ill.: Theosophical Publishing House, 1987.

Nicoll, Maurice. *Living Time*. Boston: Shambhala Publications, 1985.

O'Flaherty, Wendy Doniger. *Other People's Myths*. New York: Macmillan, 1988.

Osherman, Samuel. *Finding Our Fathers: The Unfinished Business of Manhood*. New York: Free Press, 1966.

Pearce, Joseph Chilton. *Magical Child*. New York: Bantam Books, 1977.

Priestley, J.B. *Man and Time*. London: Aldus, 1969.

Sawyer, Ruth. *The Way of the Storyteller*. New York: Viking Press, 1962.

Seed, John. *Thinking Like A Mountain*. Philadelphia: New Society Publishers, 1988.

Shedlock, Marie. *The Art of the Story-Teller*. New York: Dover, 1951.

Smith, Jimmy Neil. *Homespun: Tales from America's Favorite Storytellers*. New York: Crown Publishers, 1988.

Spencer, Paula Underwood. *Who Speaks for Wolf*. Austin, Tex.: Tribe of Two Press, 1983.

Stone, Merlin. *When God Was a Woman*. New York: Harcourt Brace Jovanovich, 1976.

Swan, Jim. *Sacred Places*. Santa Fe: Bear & Co., 1990.

Swimme, Brian. *The Universe Is a Green Dragon: A Cosmic Creation Story*. Santa Fe: Bear & Co., 1984.

Thompson, Stith. *The Folktale*. New York: Dryden Press, 1951.

Trelease, Jim. *The Read-Aloud Handbook*. New York: Penguin Books, 1979.

Ullman, Montague, and Zimmerman, Nan. *Working with Dreams*. Los Angeles: Jeremy P. Tarcher, 1979.

von Franz, Marie Louise. *The Feminine in Fairytales*. Dallas, Tex.: Spring Publications, 1972.

————. *Individuation in Fairytales*. Dallas, Tex.: Spring Publications, 1977.

————. *Interpretation of Fairytales*. Dallas, Tex.: Spring Publications, 1970.

————. *Shadow and Evil in Fairytales*. Dallas, Tex.: Spring Publications, 1974.

Williams, Strephon Kaplan. *The Jungian-Senoi Dreamwork Manual*. Berkeley, Calif.: Journey Press, 1980.

Periodicals

Gnosis: A Journal of the Western Inner Traditions. Box 14217, San Francisco, CA 94114.

Inroads: A Journal of the Male Soul. Box 14944, University Station, Minneapolis, MN 55414.

Parabola: Myth and the Quest for Meaning. Box 165, Brooklyn, NY 11202.

Shaman's Drum: A Journal of Experiential Shamanism. Box 16507, North Hollywood, CA 91615.

Audio Tapes and Other Materials

Bly, Robert. *Fairy Tales for Men and Women*. Ally Press Center, 524 Orleans Street, St. Paul, MN 55107.

The Foundation for Shamanic Studies, Box 670, Belden Station, Norwalk CT 06852

Larkin. *O'Cean*. Narada Productions, 1845 Farwell Avenue, Milwaukee, WI 53202.

Mindfolds. Mindfold, Inc. 8043 East 7th Street, Tucson, AZ 85710.

Moore, Robin. *Awakening the Hidden Storyteller*. Two cassettes (2 hours) based on the book. Available from Shambhala Lion Editions, Shambhala Publications, 300 Massachusetts Avenue, Boston, MA 02115. (617) 424-0030.

Moore, Robin. *When the Moon Is Full: Supernatural Stories from the Pennsylvania Mountains*. Groundhog Press, Box 181, Springhouse, PA 19477.

Story, Medicine. *Tales of the Eastern*

Woodlands. Yellow Moon Press,
Box 1316, Cambridge, MA 02238.
Swan, Jim. *Chanting Circle*, Snow-
goose Productions, Box 637, Mill
Valley, CA 94942.

Robin Moore is available for storytelling workshops and performances based on the material presented in this book. For information and fees, write to Groundhog Press, Box 181, Springhouse, PA 19477.

To receive a catalogue with an extensive offering of books and tapes from storytellers nationwide, contact Yellow Moon Press, Box 1316, Cambridge, MA 02238.